T0085825

# BIG IDEAS THAT CHANGED THE WORLD

# ALL CHARGED UP!

DON BROWN

AMULET BOOKS • NEW YORK

The artwork for this book was created digitally.

Library of Congress Control Number 2023936451

ISBN 978-1-4197-6673-2


Edited by Howard W. Reeves
Book design by Chelsea Hunter

Published in 2024 by Amulet Books, an imprint of ABRAMS. 

Printed and bound in China

10 9 8 7 6 5 4 3 2 1

**ABRAMS** The Art of Books
195 Broadway, New York, NY 10007
abramsbooks.com

For Deborah, the light of my life

**Note to Reader**: Unless otherwise noted, quotation marks signal actual quotes.

Imagine this: A monstrous cyclone rushes over tumbling seas toward the great Indian city of Calcutta. The city is doomed. Or is it? At sea, between the storm and the city, is our hero. He pours a special potion on the troubled water, calming the waves, taming the storm, and saving the city!

What is this magic potion?
Hair oil!
Fantastic, yes?
It is a story I wrote. My name is Jagadish Chandra Bose. Some people call me the "Father of Bengali Science Fiction."

BANGLADESH
INDIA
AUSTRALIA

And it is a Real Big Idea Science Story I want to share with you, of how a colossal power greater than any cyclone was uncovered, tamed, and grew into something we all can't live without . . .

At first, electricity was all fear and mystery.
Jagged and dazzling lightning ripped the sky or exploded into the ground, appearing and disappearing with only myth and legend to explain it. Electricity's role in making lightning was unknown.

Unknown, too, was why the touch of certain fish or eels produced a shock. The idea of an "electric" eel was not even considered. How could it be if electricity was unknown?
YOW!
HA!
ZAP

Many, many years passed until 600 BCE, when a Greek mathematician and astronomer, Thales of Miletus, observed the peculiar behavior of amber.

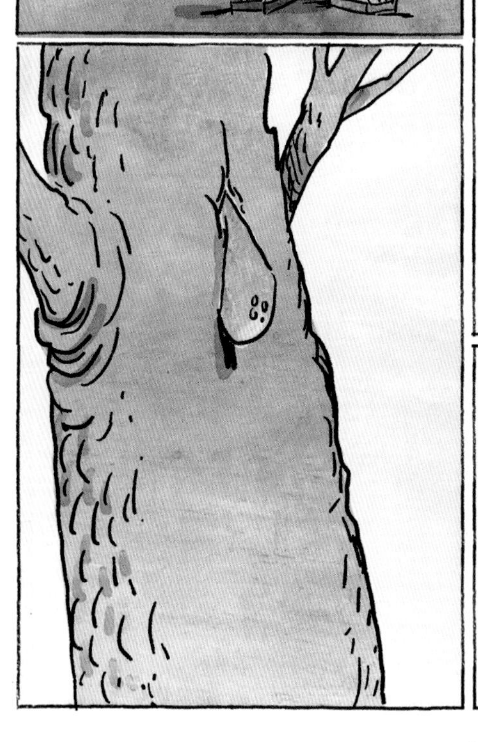

Amber is the goop that oozes out of tree trunks and over millions of years fossilizes into a gem-like substance.

When rubbed with a cloth, amber has the strange ability to attract lightweight objects like feathers, straw, or leaves.

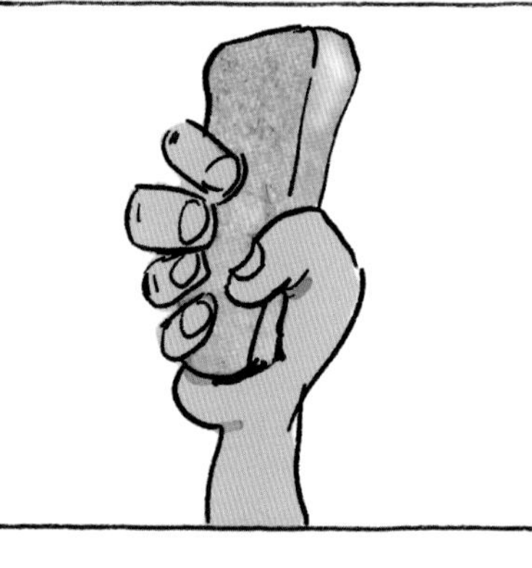

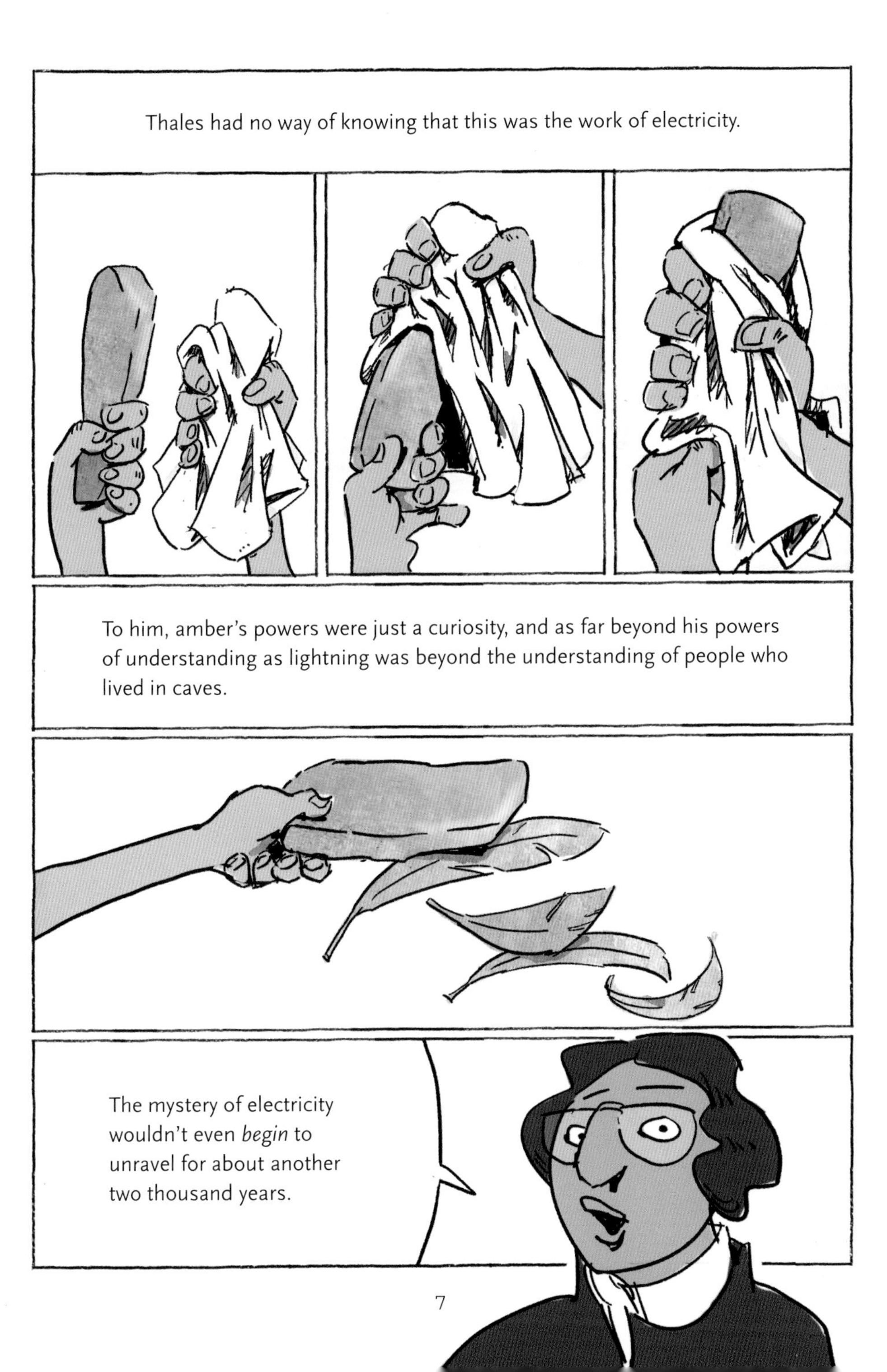
Thales had no way of knowing that this was the work of electricity.
To him, amber's powers were just a curiosity, and as far beyond his powers of understanding as lightning was beyond the understanding of people who lived in caves.
The mystery of electricity wouldn't even *begin* to unravel for about another two thousand years.

In 1600, William Gilbert was the doctor for England's Queen Elizabeth I.
COUGH!
HMMM
When not tending to the queen, he turned his attention to cloth-stroked amber and its power to attract feathers and straw.
It reminded him of the power of magnets to attract certain metals. Gilbert called the power *electric*, inspired by the Greek word for amber, *elektron*. He came to believe there was an invisible power that he called *electrical effluvia*.
EFFLUVIA

Gilbert experimented with other materials. After rubbing them, he placed a small metal needle balanced on a pinhead nearby. If the needle swung toward it or away from it, much the way a compass needle turns in the presence of a magnet, Gilbert declared the rubbed object to have "electricity." (Today, we call an electric charge on an object *static electricity*.)

In any case, others, like Englishmen Francis Hauksbee and Stephen Gray, built on Gilbert's Big Idea to startling effect.

In the early 1700s, Francis Hauksbee made a hollow glass sphere, pumped out all the air, and connected it to a crank. He spun the sphere and rubbed it with his hands, making an electric charge that glowed with an eerie blue light.

Stephen Gray amazed people with his "Flying Boy" demonstration, where he suspended a boy on silk ropes and connected him to a Hauksbee-like device. The boy's hair would stand on end and sparks leaped off the tip of his nose.

The cool demonstrations of Hauksbee and Gray aside, the work of Professor Pieter van Musschenbroek in Leyden, Holland, took a more serious turn. It was all well and good to create an electric charge, he thought, but what about storing it, so that it could be available at a later time?

In around 1739, he suspected an electric charge could be stored in a container of something like water or milk. The professor lined a glass jug with metal foil inside and out, added water, then capped it with a cork.

Then he pierced the cork with a brass ball and rod connected to a metal chain extending to the foil at the bottom of the jug. Musschenbroek set a Hauksbee-like machine spinning, generating an electric charge that was sent by wire to the jug.

ZAP

Although it was painfully earned, Musschenbroek proved electricity could be stored.

His discovery became known as the *Leyden jar* . . . I guess *Musschenbroek jar* was just too much of a mouthful.

News of the Leyden jar spread everywhere, including across the Atlantic Ocean to England's colonies, where it caught the attention of a successful publisher and self-taught scientist, Benjamin Franklin.

Franklin tried all kinds of experiments with the Leyden jar, and he, too, learned the shocking lesson of electrical power.

An unexpected spark delivered a . . .
". . . universal blow throughout my whole body."
Ignoring his painful experience, Franklin decided to fly a kite in a thunderstorm to prove that lightning was electric— an idea that wasn't widely accepted at the time.

On a muggy afternoon in 1852, Franklin and his son launched a kite into a lightning-scarred sky. Attached to the kite was a foot-long metal wire. A metal key hung from the string. The kite string ended in a Leyden jar.

A bit reckless, no?

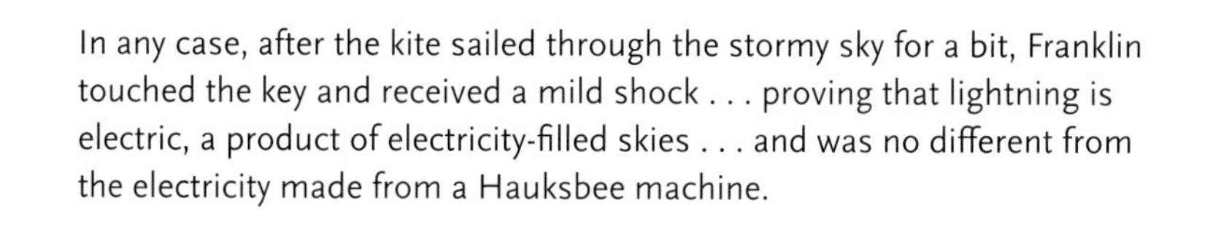
In any case, after the kite sailed through the stormy sky for a bit, Franklin touched the key and received a mild shock . . . proving that lightning is electric, a product of electricity-filled skies . . . and was no different from the electricity made from a Hauksbee machine.

Yes, I know what you're thinking . . . if the kite was never *struck* by lightning, how could Franklin declare that lightning was electric?

He made a reasonable scientific conclusion from the evidence.

Besides, at the same time as Franklin's kite-flying experiment, French scientists also tested Ben's theory about lightning.

Instead of using a kite, they erected a tall metal rod with a jar at its bottom to collect a lightning strike's electricity.

A storm arrived. The rod was struck . . .

*Voilá*—electricity!

A Swedish scientist should have left it at that, but instead he tried his own experiment with lightning, holding aloft a wire-tipped pole during a thunderstorm.

Lightning struck the pole, killing him and reminding us that if lightning had struck Franklin's kite, America would likely have lost one of its most important Founding Fathers.

Here's my advice: Don't experiment with lightning . . . it's too dangerous!

Franklin's energies would soon be directed toward American independence—but not before he had the Big Idea that electricity was a kind of invisible fluid. If an object had the "normal" amount of it, it had no charge. If it had too much, it was positive. If it had too little, it was negative. Ben reasoned that too much—positive—electricity would naturally flow to where it was lacking—a negative charge—to make the thing equal, or "normal."

He called the wire that carried electricity a "conduit," and the collection of electricity-storing vessels "batteries" after the term for a collection of cannons. Positive and negative electricity, conduit, and batteries are terms still used today.

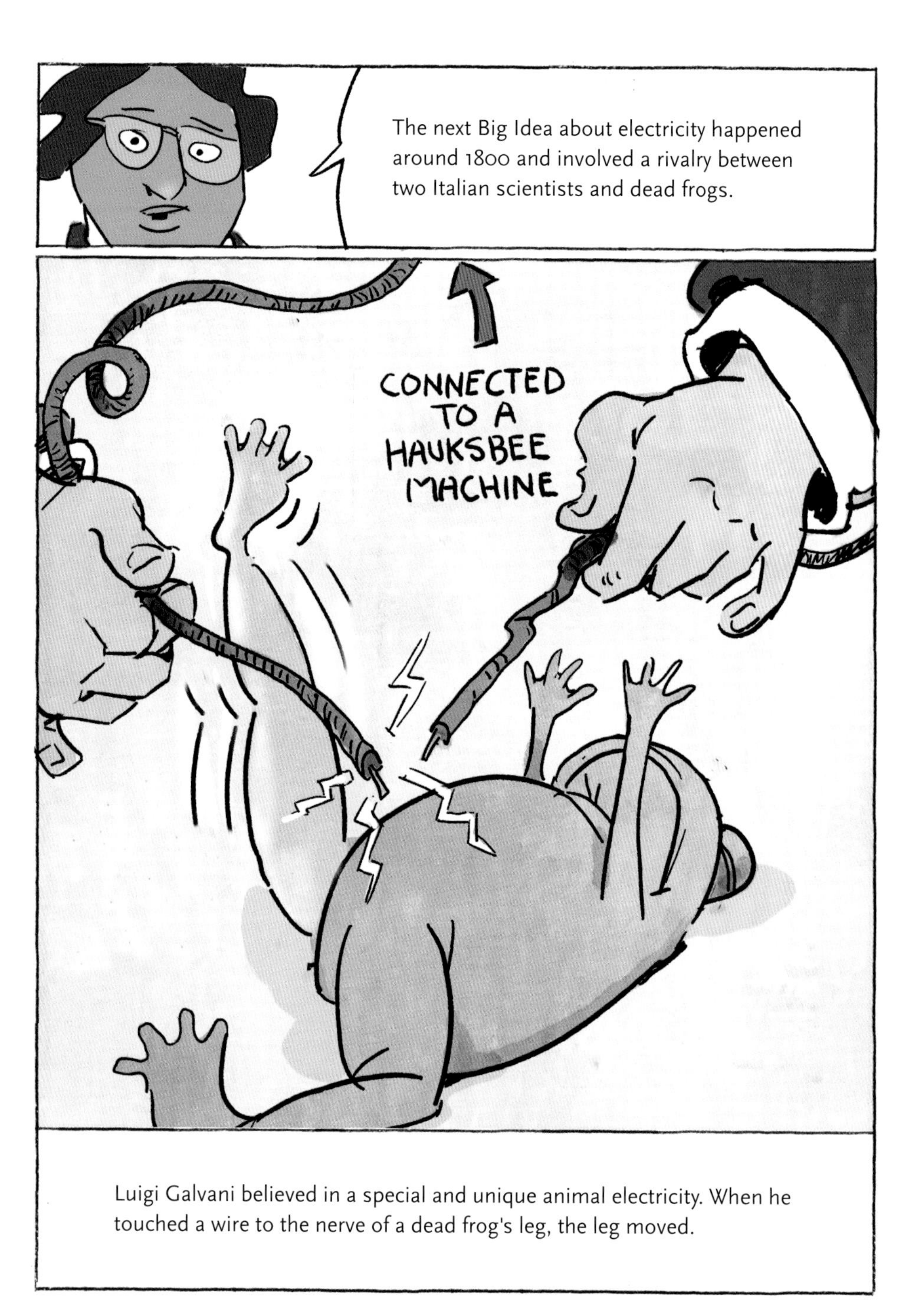
The next Big Idea about electricity happened around 1800 and involved a rivalry between two Italian scientists and dead frogs.
CONNECTED TO A HAUKSBEE MACHINE
Luigi Galvani believed in a special and unique animal electricity. When he touched a wire to the nerve of a dead frog's leg, the leg moved.

But when he hung a dead frog from a wire and then touched the frog's leg nerve without an apparent electrical charge, the dead frog's leg still moved! Since there was no outside source of electricity, Galvani concluded that special animal electricity *inside* the frog made the leg move.

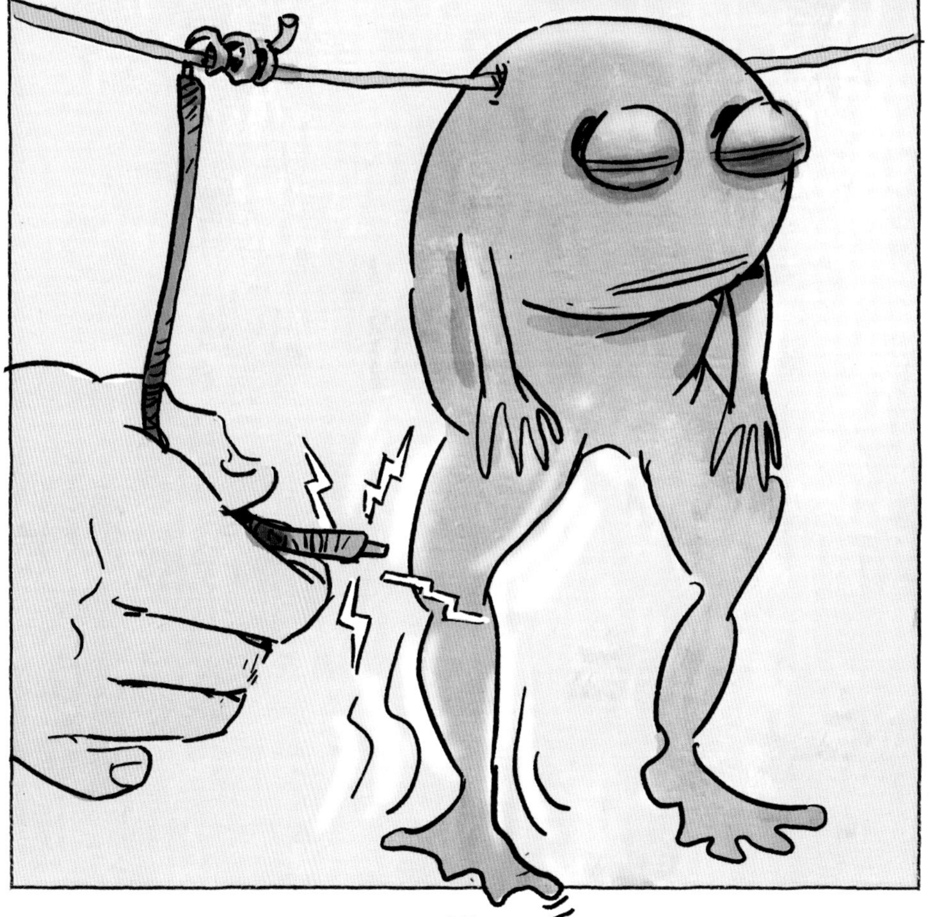

It seemed like a sensible idea, but Alessandro Volta didn't buy it. Oh yes, there were eels and fish that could make electricity, but theirs was like all other electricity, not some special, unusual *animal* electricity.

Volta thought and thought.

He remembered Galvani's experiment had only three parts: the dead frog, the brass wire it hung from, and the iron wire Galvani used to touch the creature's nerve.

Volta concluded that the electricity must have come from *just the metal wires*!

But how could he prove different metals alone could make electricity?

Volta remembered that if he touched his tongue with two small pieces of copper and zinc, he felt a slight tingling . . . *as if tasting electricity*.

Volta had a Big Idea that if two small pieces of metal created a little bit of electricity, then many small pieces would create greater electricity.

He piled zinc and copper disks, sandwiching saltwater-soaked paper between them to mimic the saliva on his tongue when he "tasted" electricity.

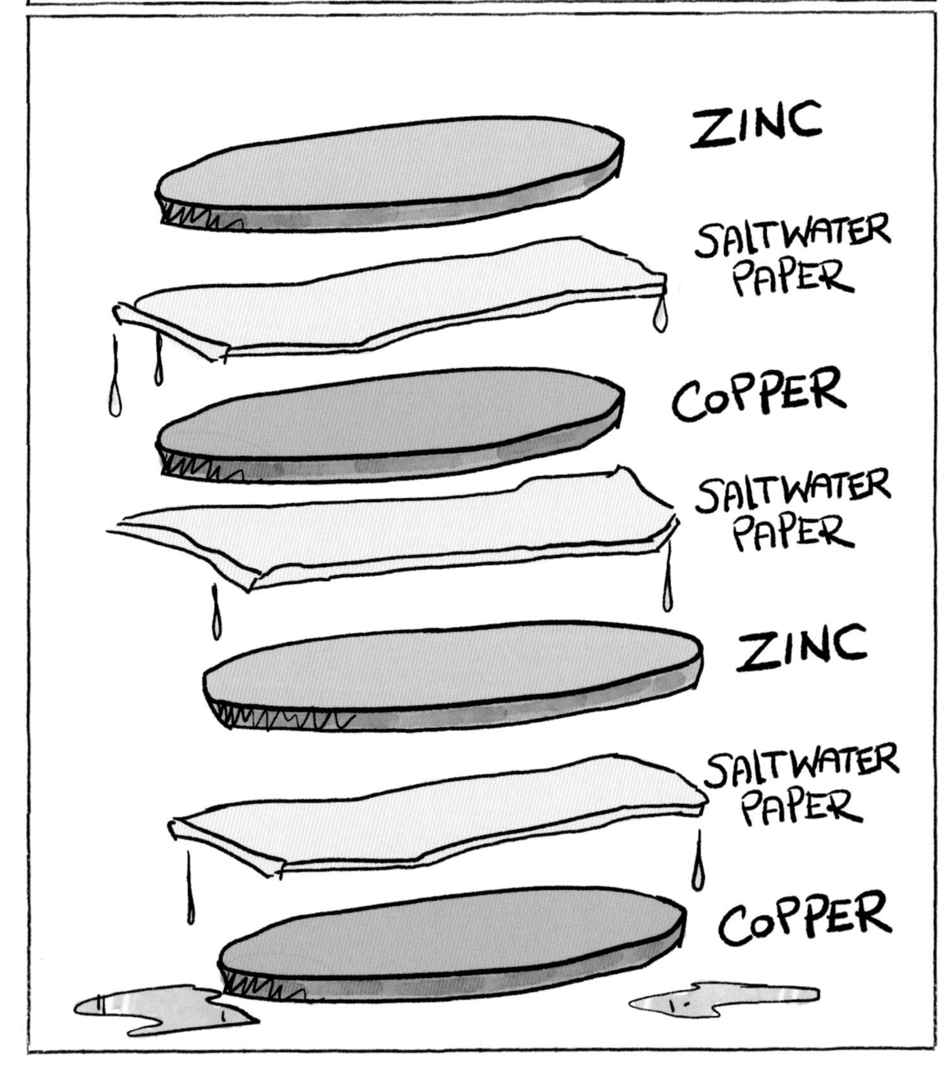

When he attached wires to the pile, Volta discovered a *continuous* flow of electricity!

Where a Leyden jar would unload its electricity in a burst, Volta's pile would release electricity in a river-like flow, or current, as long the saltwater-metal sandwich didn't dry out or the metals didn't corrode.

Volta had invented the first real battery!

The prospect of a steady stream of electricity . . . *electrified* the world . . . sorry for the bad pun. In any case, Volta's "pile" excited scientists everywhere.

It was . . .

Volta's discovery also proved Galvani wrong—there was no special or unique animal electricity.

But in a strange twist, the steady current created by Volta's battery became known as *Galvanic*.

That doesn't seem fair!

Still, we measure the electric force in a current in *volts*, to which I say, "Good for you, Alessandro."

But let me for a moment return to my other interest, the world of science fiction. Galvani's nephew Giovanni Aldini continued to explore electricity and living things. He applied electricity to all sorts of dead animals, making them move and twist. When he did the same to a dead person . . . well, let's just say that people who saw the gruesome display never forgot it.

And news of it spread, reaching the ears of Englishwoman Mary Shelley. It inspired her to write the tale of a scientist using electricity to bring a dead person back to life. You might have heard of it—*Frankenstein*.

It's been said that Shelley modeled the scientist in her book not on Aldini but on Humphrey Davy, a well-known English chemistry scientist of the day. And Humphrey Davy indeed plays a role in our story of electricity.

He showed that electricity could break up chemical compounds into their individual pieces. For example, running a current into water would result in releasing the components of water: hydrogen and oxygen.

He was also something of a showman.

In 1801, he connected a basement filled with two thousand volta-like batteries to a pair of carbon rods, then brought the rods close together.

Electricity leaped—or arced—the three-inch space between the rods, making a great, continuous spark and bright light.

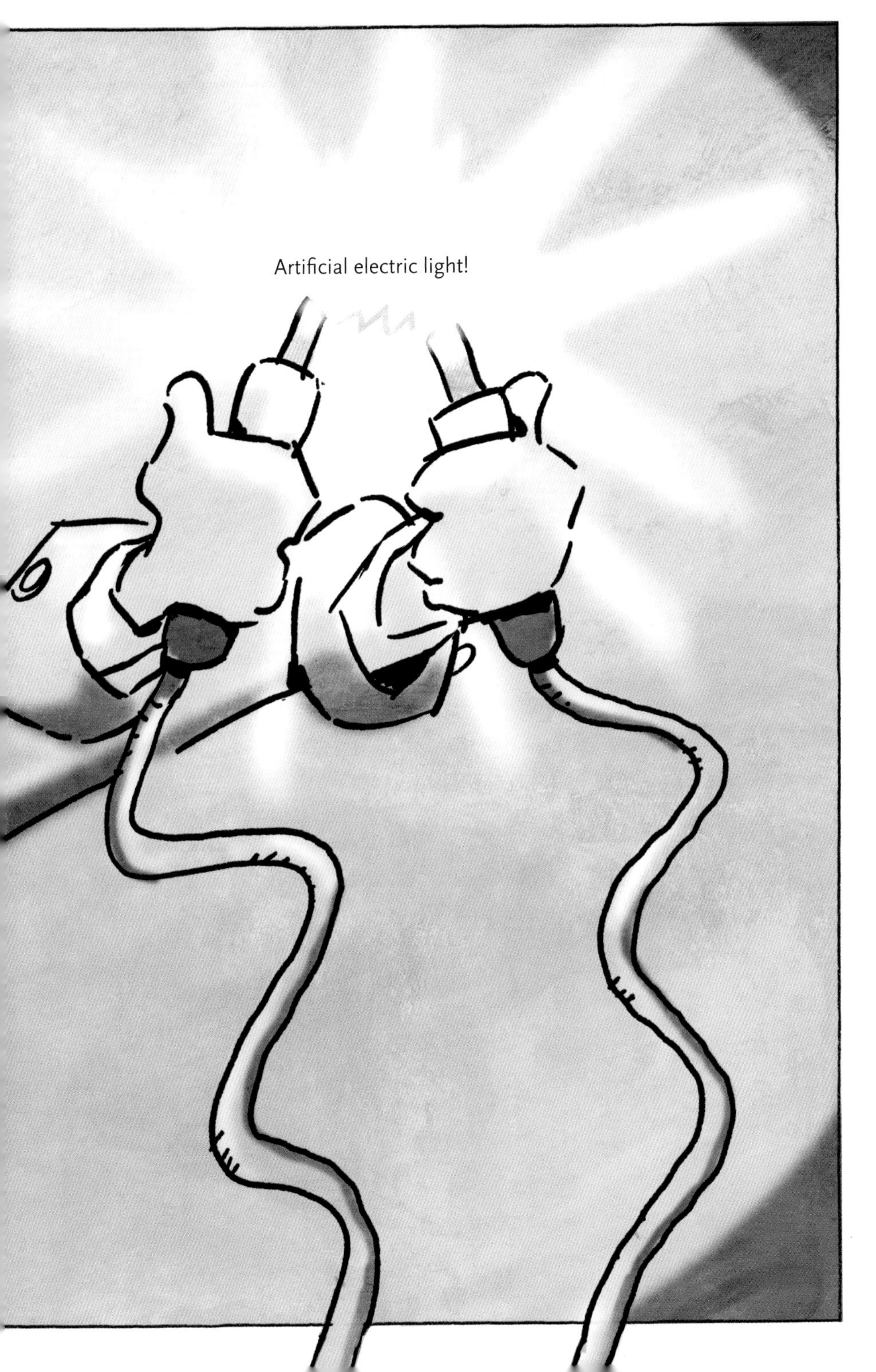
Artificial electric light!

Davy didn't recognize the arc lamp as a Big Idea. He saw his demonstration as more of a parlor trick to astonish viewers than a serious experiment worthy of further study. Besides, the electric arc lamp had many shortcomings. The intense light was much too bright for indoor use, and not everyone could fill their basements with batteries. And in 1801, there was no way to make—or generate—enough electricity to feed the arc lamp for long stretches of time.

The arc lamp would stay a curiosity for decades until its drawbacks were overcome, and they were sometimes employed as streetlamps. By then, another electric light invention would overshadow the arc lamp . . . but I'm getting ahead of myself.

In the meantime, Davy discovered that adding acid to a metal stack of a battery made it work better, a breakthrough made at the same time by Danish scientist Hans Christian Ørsted.

But Ørsted is better remembered for his experiments with electricity and magnetism.
"An attempt should be made to see if electricity . . . has any action of a magnet."
Once, during the middle of a lecture, Ørsted had a Big Idea. To the puzzlement of his listeners, he abruptly walked out on his own talk, going directly to his laboratory.
!

Ørsted had the idea to place a compass *below* a wire. A compass is simply a thin magnet on a pivot that is known for aligning itself to the Earth's magnetic field. But it will also respond to any near magnetism.

When Ørsted passed electricity through the wire, the compass turned.

If he placed the compass *above* the electric wire, the compass swung in the opposite direction.

It didn't matter if the electrified wire was gold, brass, or silver. It didn't matter if wood, glass, or metal separated the compass from the wire. The electric wire made the compass swing.

The compass was responding to an invisible magnetic force created by the electric wire.

It was a simple but potent discovery, exciting scientists and engineers around the world. Expanding on Ørsted, they learned that the more powerful the electrical charge in the wire, the greater the magnetism.

With that in mind, American Joseph Henry, in the 1820s, took wire insulated with silk taken from his wife's discarded dresses and coiled it around a piece of iron. When the wire was attached to a battery, it became a powerful electromagnet.

2,000 POUNDS
Using hundreds of feet of coils, Henry eventually created huge horseshoe-shaped electromagnets that could lift a ton of metal.
Amazing, yes?

Needing a secretary to help him with his writing while he recovered, he hired a young man with a reputation for fine penmanship: Michael Faraday.

It would later be said that Humphrey Davy's greatest discovery was Michael Faraday.

He was no fancy-pants son of wealth and privilege; Faraday's father was an unsuccessful blacksmith. His poor family lived for a time on the road to Newgate Prison; condemned prisoners were driven past the house on the way to being hanged.

By age thirteen, Faraday's formal education had ended, and he was apprenticed to a bookbinder to learn the craft of bookmaking—joining printed sheets to a hardcover.

The surroundings suited the endlessly curious Faraday.

Although hired as a secretary, Faraday soon became Davy's scientific associate. The job came with lodging at the Royal Society, a scientific organization that Davy headed for several years. Employment also came with a supply of coal and candles.

Eventually, Faraday turned his mind to the mysteries of electricity . . . and the connection between it and magnetism.

He knew electricity created magnetism—Henry had demonstrated that—but what about . . .

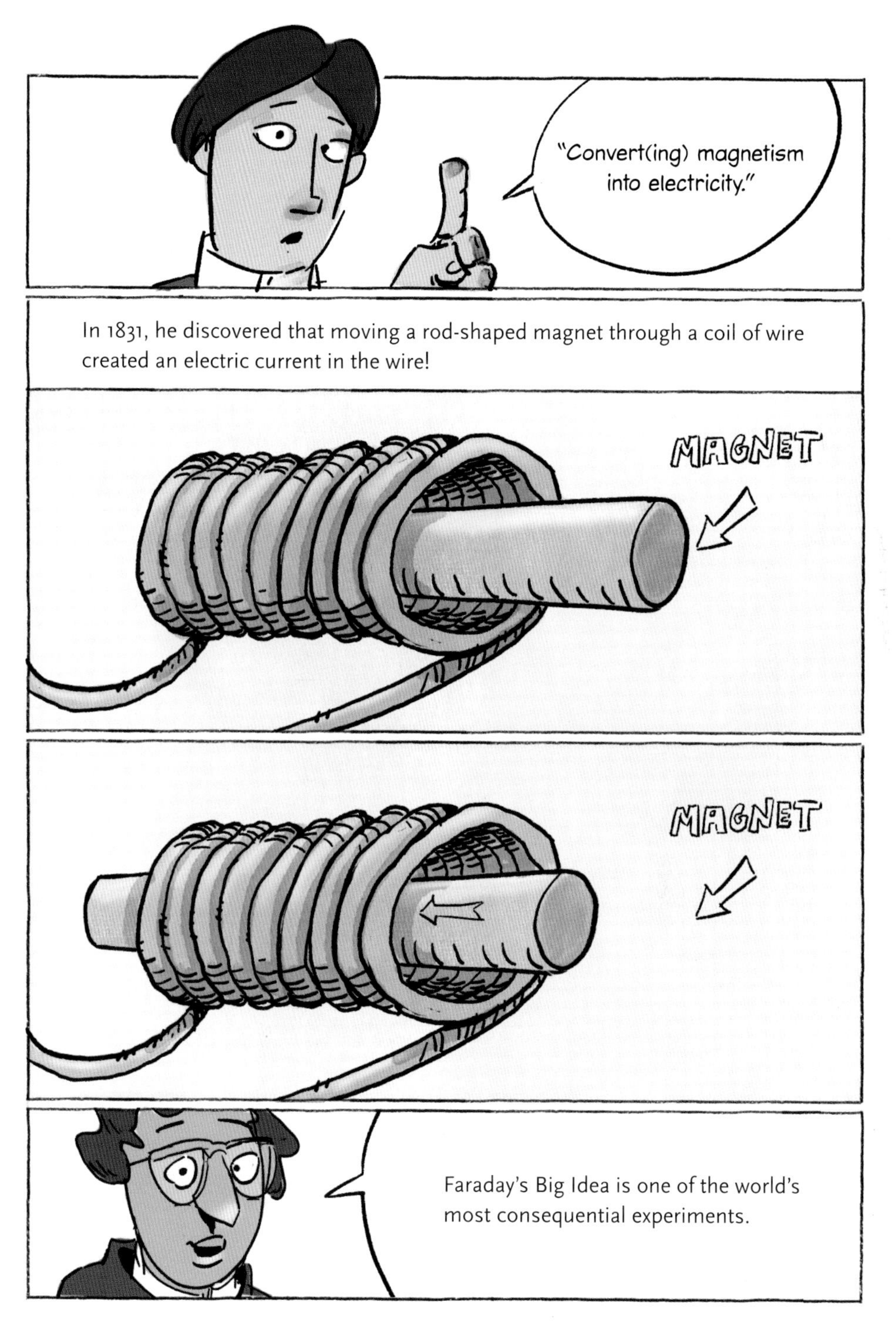
"Convert(ing) magnetism into electricity."
In 1831, he discovered that moving a rod-shaped magnet through a coil of wire created an electric current in the wire!
MAGNET
MAGNET
Faraday's Big Idea is one of the world's most consequential experiments.

But the electric current was only momentary. How could he create a continuous electrical current?

He connected a copper disk to wires and placed a magnet over the disk.

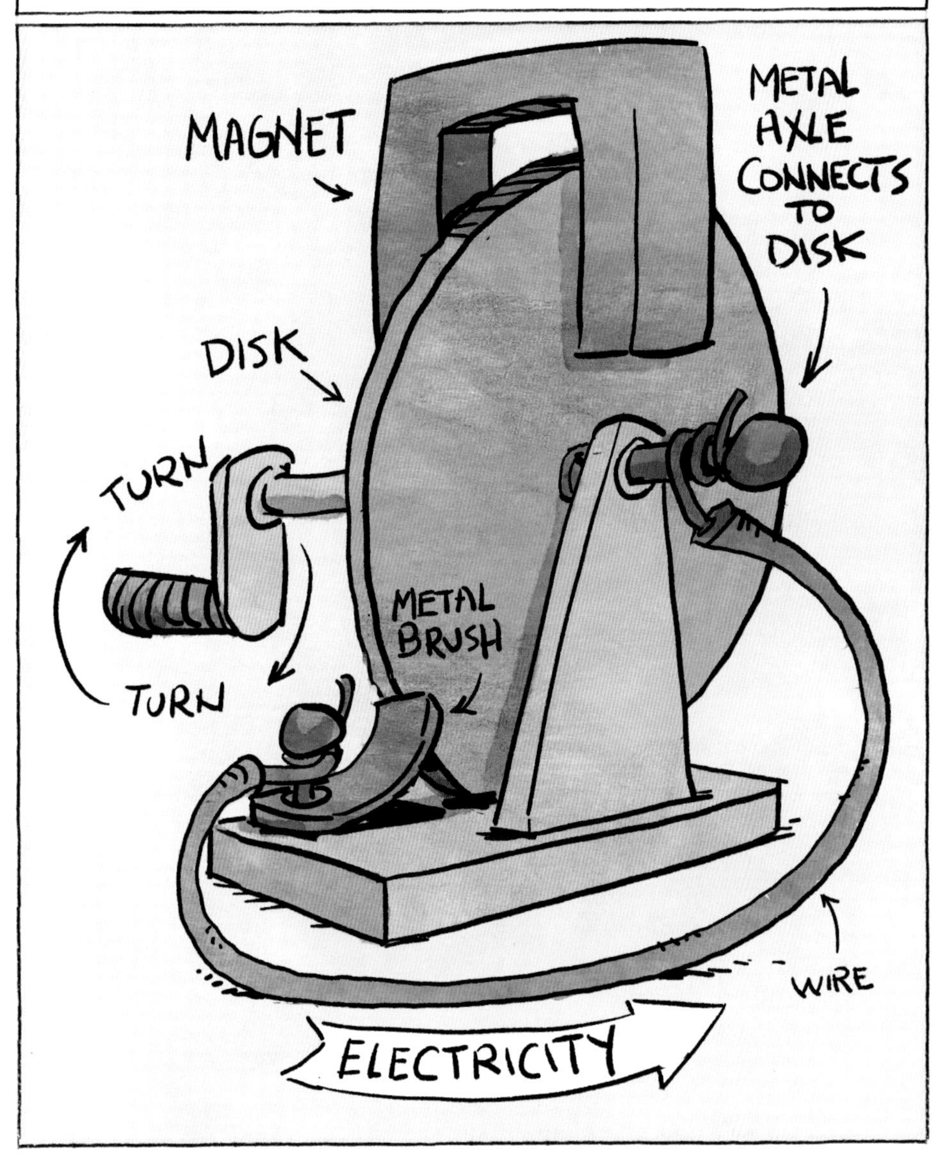

Rotating the disk created a continuous flow of electricity that would continue as long as the disk turned . . . a big improvement over batteries that would wear out or die, limiting their electrical current.

At that moment, the Age of Steam—where machines labored by mechanical means—ended, and the Age of Electricity was born.

Fatafati, yes?

In a way, every time you flip a light switch, your fingertip is touching Michael Faraday's.

Oh, here's another Faraday idea . . . you can decide whether it's big or small.

He was smitten by science and believed others, especially children, should be, too. In 1825, he started making scientific presentations to kids. They charmed everyone and became a holiday staple. Other scientists have continued Faraday's Christmas Lectures for children to this day.

Getting back to electricity . . . Soon, it was no longer confined to scientific labs and became part of everyday life.

American Samuel Morse created the telegraph.

Using a key that connected and disconnected an electric circuit, he could send a series of short and long clicks—dots and dashes—over a wire. A combination of dots and dashes was assigned to each letter of the alphabet. A collection of dots and dashes could spell words and create a message.

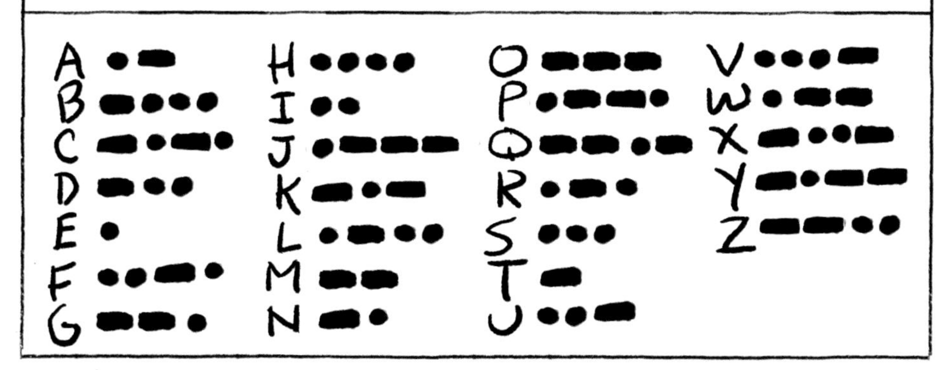

Messages that might have taken days or weeks to arrive now could be sent in moments.
MAIL
In 1844, Morse sent the first telegraph message from Baltimore, Maryland, to Washington, D.C.: "What hath God wrought!" Hmm . . . I'm not quite sure what he meant by that.
"WHAT HATH GOD WROUGHT"

Soon there were telegraph poles and wires everywhere.

By 1861, the Western Union Telegraph Company became the first to string telegraph wires across North America.

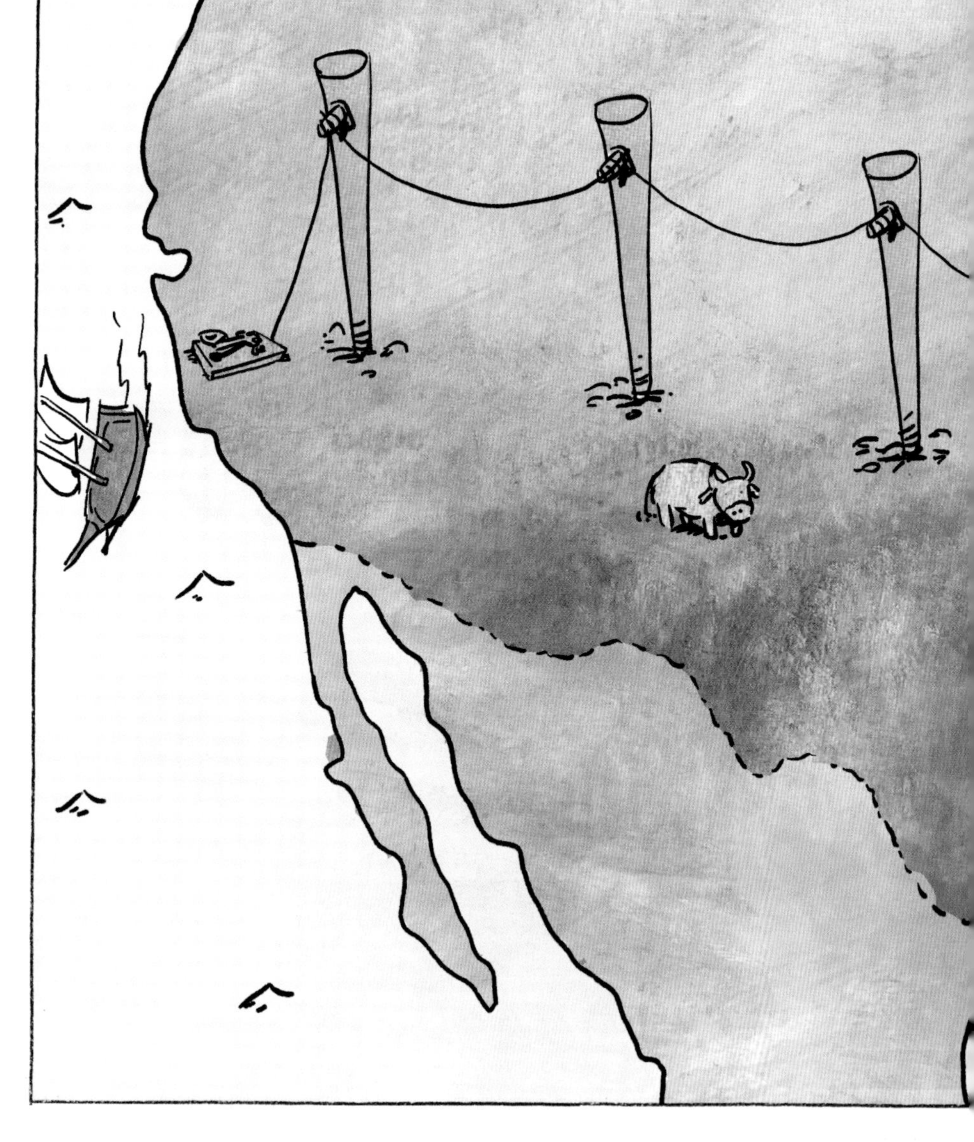

American Cyrus Field had the Big Idea to connect North America and Europe by way of a telegraph line laid on the floor of the Atlantic Ocean. It took a couple of tries to get the system to work, but by 1866, people could send messages between North America and Europe.

In 1875, Alexander Graham Bell and partner Thomas Watson devised a way to transform a human voice into electrical impulses. Then they sent them over wire to a receiver that changed the impulses back into sound: the telephone!

Lewis Latimer helped Bell draw the telephone plans for a patent, an official government recognition that an original Big Idea belongs to the inventor. With a patent, the inventor can charge money for people to use that invention.

Elsewhere, Granville T. Woods invented the "third rail," an electrified rail running alongside train tracks. A special device connected the train to the rail, allowing the train's electric engine to draw electricity and power the train. He also devised improved railroad brakes, one of his roughly fifty inventions. He was compared to Thomas Edison.

You don't know Thomas Edison?
He is America's best-known inventor.

He improved the telegraph, created the phonograph, and helped develop motion pictures. Of course, people say his greatest invention was the . . .
TELEGRAPH
PHONOGRAPH
MOTION PICTURES

. . . electric lightbulb.

Not only did the lightbulb transform a world "lit by fire," it started a scientific rivalry between two big thinkers that would change the way everyone on the planet lives.

But first, let me tell you about lightbulbs, so named because they resembled tulip bulbs.

Sometimes when electricity passes through a thin material, the material will heat up and glow. Think about how the elements in toasters glow. The ability to create light from a heated object is called *incandescence*.

By the late nineteenth century, many people were racing to invent a practical, electric incandescent lamp, including British scientist Joseph Swan—responsible for developing the first incandescent lights used to illuminate homes and public buildings in London—and New Jersey's own Thomas Edison.

The stumbling block was practicality.

All kinds of materials and objects, including beard hairs, were tried as glowing material, or *filament*, but they all melted or burned out quickly, making them useless for everyday household use.

Edison and his assistants at his Menlo Park, New Jersey, laboratory tried removing all the air from the lightbulbs, believing that the filament would burn slower if there was no air surrounding it.

Finally, in 1879, Edison and his assistants tried a thin bamboo and carbon filament. They placed it into a bulb, sucked out the air, and sent electricity streaming through the bamboo.

It glowed for hour after hour after hour.

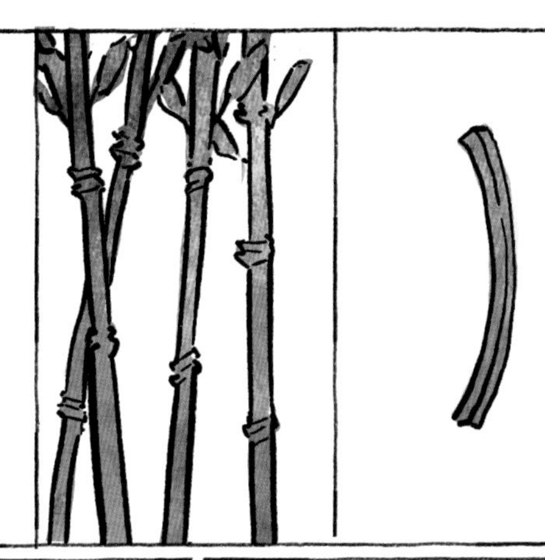

It was a great discovery, but people weren't sure it was right to call Edison the "inventor" of the lightbulb.

Basic understanding of incandescent light was well known before Edison. Just ask Joseph Swan. Edison's contribution was important, but was he deserving of being honored as the lightbulb's *inventor*? The argument still rages.

And Swan . . . he ended up going into business with Edison, forming the Edison and Swan Electric Light Company.

Meanwhile, Edison protected his inventions with government patents. Helping Edison secure patents was Lewis Latimer . . . yes, the same Lewis Latimer who helped Alexander Graham Bell. Latimer would also invent a more durable and longer-lasting lightbulb filament.

What Edison undoubtedly deserves credit for is inventing a *whole system of electric lighting*. He saw a world of wires that connected central, electricity-generating stations to homes and businesses, and where special meters kept track of how much electricity users consumed and charged them accordingly. He even came up with the screw-in lightbulb.

METER
METER
METER
And Edison envisioned a world where electricity wouldn't be limited to lightbulbs:
". . . the same wire that brings the light to you . . . will also bring power and heat . . . you may cook your food."

STATUE OF LIBERTY NOT YET BUILT
MANHATTAN
To prove his vision for an electrical system, he promised to light up a square mile of New York City.

PEARL ST
WATER ST.
BROOKLYN BRIDGE
NOT YET BUILT
BROOKLYN

He built the world's first power plant at Pearl Street in Lower Manhattan. In it, he installed six dynamos—electricity-making machines based on Michael Faraday's ideas—with the power to light about 7,200 lightbulbs. Each coal-fired, steam-driven dynamo weighed about 27 tons.

No wonder they were called "Jumbos."

Working at night, Edison's men buried 100,000 feet of wire, or conduit, beneath the streets to carry the electricity from the Jumbos to neighboring buildings.

The preparations took four years.

It was a bold and untested plan.
"All our devices and parts . . . were homemade . . . Our men were without central power experience . . . what might happen on turning a big current into the conductors under the streets . . . no one could say."

On September 4, 1882, Edison threw a switch, sending electricity coursing from the dynamos to the business offices of financial leader J. P. Morgan.

About four hundred lightbulbs came to life.

"They're on!"
"The light was soft, mellow, and grateful to the eye."
Soon, about two thousand electric lightbulbs shined in Lower Manhattan.
Oh, and in case you wondered . . . each newly lit lightbulb cost about a dollar each.
That doesn't sound like much, but think about this: A laborer who buried Edison's wires probably earned only about *two dollars a day!*

Immediately, there was an impatient and widespread demand for the soft, mellow, and pleasing light.
But there was a problem.
It gets a little complicated, but I know you can handle it.
There are two different kinds of electricity: DC and AC.
*DC* stands for *direct current*, which mean the electricity moves in one direction, like water spilling down a stream.

Nearly everyone believed AC was impractical. If we return to our comparison to a stream, it's obvious that flowing water can spin a wheel, which in turn can do something useful like saw a log or grind grain. How do you make a wheel useful if the water goes one way and then the other?

They believed AC electricity could never light a bulb, or power an electric meter, or run a motor.

Edison said of AC's usefulness: "Impractical."

But Edison and the others were wrong.

And the man most responsible for proving Edison and the others wrong was Nikola Tesla.

As a child, he noticed tiny sparks as he stroked his cat. His fascination with the static charge in the cat's fur helped set him on a lifetime of exploring electricity.

Tesla moved from his Eastern European home to America, worked for Edison for a while, then struck out on his own, not always successfully. Then, with a burst of creative energy, he invented a workable AC electric motor . . . and along with it, proved AC current could be as useful as DC.

It addressed the problem I hinted at earlier: DC current petered out after only about a mile, like a stream drying up.

Oh, there were other ways around it, like using a thicker wire. But extending the electricity just a few miles required a wire as "thick as a man's leg!"

That clearly wasn't workable.

So, Edison envisioned having smoky, coal-burning power plants every mile.

Hmm . . . I don't like that.

And what about small towns and farm country? There wouldn't be enough customers to support the construction of an expensive power plant.

On the other hand, AC current could travel for great distances, and a single AC power plant could supply electricity for homes and businesses for miles around.

Savvy businesspeople took notice. One of them, George Westinghouse, became AC current's biggest promoter. He even teamed up with Nikola Tesla.
But Edison had his reputation and money invested in a future of DC electricity, and he fought Westinghouse and Tesla at every turn. It came to be known as the War of the Currents.
WAR of the CURRENTS

Edison's supporters pointed out the safety of DC compared to AC.
And it was true: DC current was low *voltage* (remember Volta?) with small risk of harming people.
AC was high voltage and had the potential for hurting people.
DC
AC
It was on this difference that the war took a grisly turn.
DC proponents promoted the dangers of AC with demonstrations where stray dogs, calves, and horses were electrocuted!

Despite the awful and horrible theatrics, people learned AC could be smartly and safely handled.

The unofficial War of the Currents ended unofficially in 1895, when engineers used the falling water at Niagara Falls to spin AC generators that sent electricity about twenty miles away to the city of Buffalo.

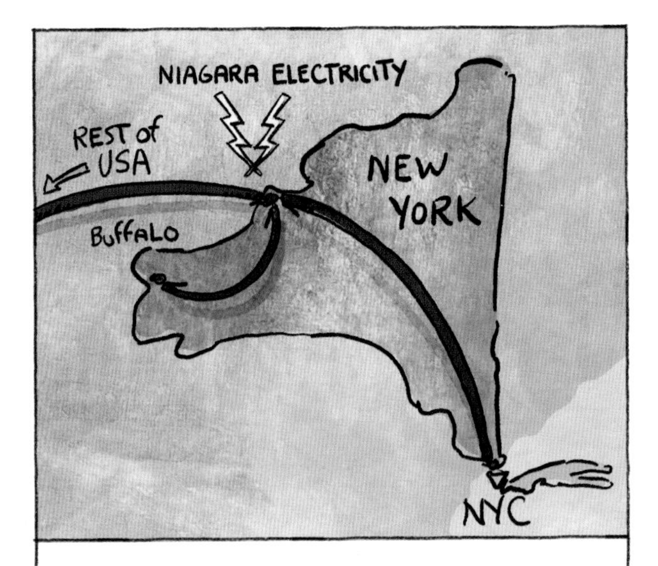


Soon, Niagara Falls supplied electricity to New York City, four hundred miles away. By 1905, 10 percent of all the electrical power in the United States was generated at Niagara Falls. When a second power plant was added, Niagara Falls produced electrical power equal to all the power then being produced elsewhere across America.

With the ready usefulness of high-voltage AC electricity proven, AC lines began to crisscross the world. But DC didn't disappear; it's still useful and needed. Ways were found to change, or adapt, AC current to DC current when necessary. For a variety of technical reasons, your personal computer runs on DC current.

Some power plants mimicked Niagara Falls and used waterpower to turn blades connected to the magnetic shaft. Dams were built to harness the power of flowing water. Others resembled Edison's Pearl Street Power Station and used steam to turn the magnetic shaft. Most of the largest power plants today are steam generators, burning coal or oil to heat water into steam.

Atomic energy has been exploited to make electricity by using nuclear fission to generate heat to produce steam.

Oh, nuclear fission?

Fission is the process of splitting an atom in two. No, not with a sharp knife, but by using complicated science.

In the 1930s, scientist Lise Meitner helped other scientists understand how fission worked. But when it came to recognizing and awarding people for their great work regarding fission, Meitner was left out.

That wasn't fair, so I wanted to remember her here.

What's more, when the waves hit a wire, it makes an electrical current in the wire. Yes, it's a weak current, but it's still there.

To the audience, being able to ring the bell without any connecting wires was like . . . *magic*.

News of Lodge's *magic* perked up the ears of many, including . . . me.

I discovered a much better way to detect or receive the signal over a longer distance than Mr. Lodge could.
In 1895, I was able to transmit a signal about a mile.
It was called a "marvel."
I might add byapok—thoroughly awesome.

People were thrilled by the *possibilities*! If you could ring a bell across long distances without wires, then it stands to reason that you could operate a telegraph across long distances without a wire. Ships at sea could finally receive reports of bad weather or sailing hazards, or cry for help when in distress—not unimportant benefits for a world dependent on ships for moving people and goods.

Guglielmo Marconi understood as much and set out to send long-distance signals. He kept at it, lengthening the distance: 2 miles, 12 miles, 186 miles.

In 1901, Marconi flew a kite attached to a copper wire high above Newfoundland, an island east of Canada, and captured a signal sent from England, 2,300 miles away!

A great achievement, yes.
In time, voices could be transmitted through the air.

NEWFOUNDLAND

He has been hailed as the inventor of radio.

But he'd used discoveries of others to send his signals.

And his transmissions were not the first.

Is he rightfully called a great *inventor*?

What of Lodge? What of me?

Oh well, let others argue. I'm happy to have a played a role in electromagnetic waves that are the heart of radio, television, cell phones, Bluetooth, and Wi-Fi!

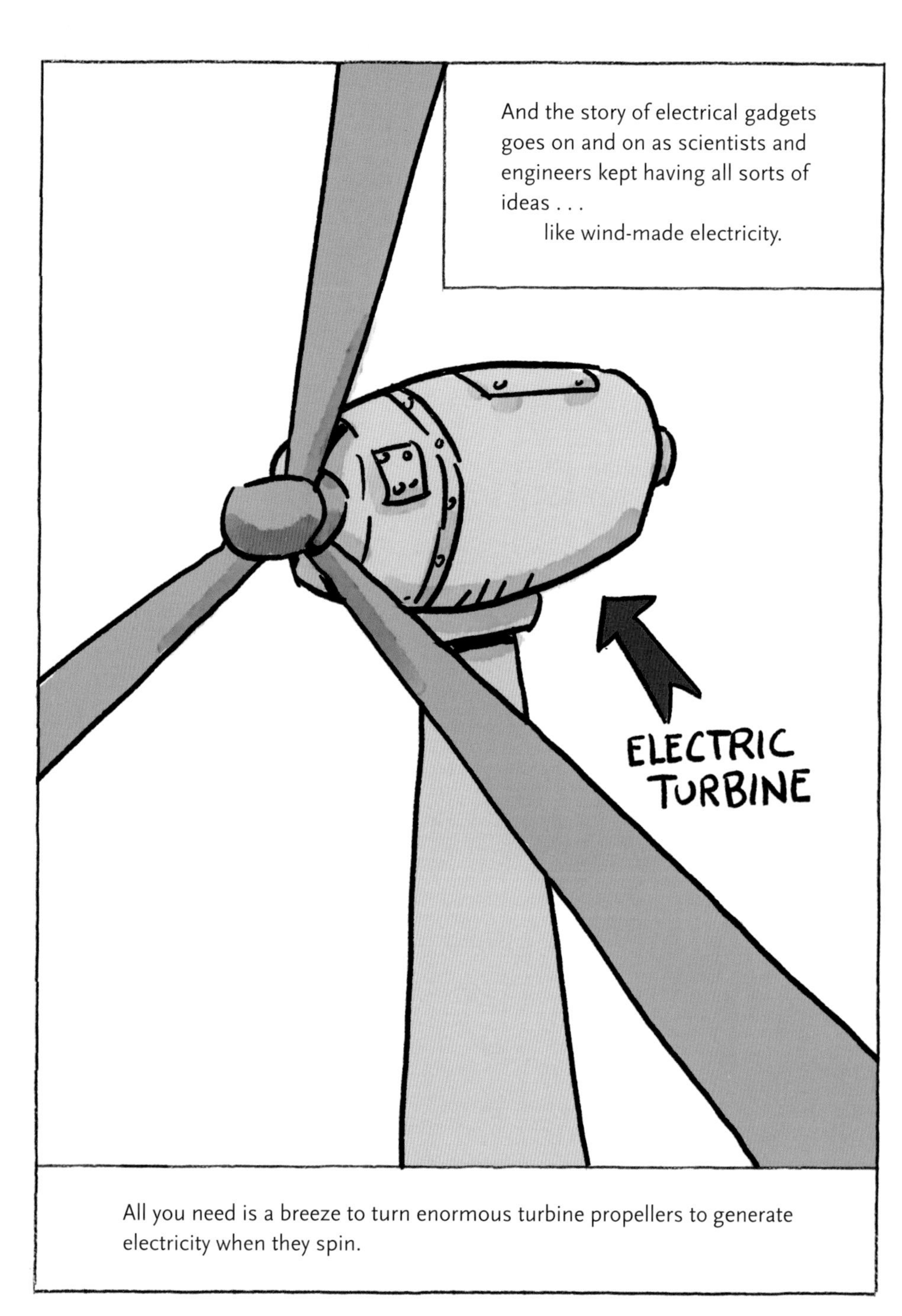
And the story of electrical gadgets goes on and on as scientists and engineers kept having all sorts of ideas . . .
like wind-made electricity.
ELECTRIC TURBINE
All you need is a breeze to turn enormous turbine propellers to generate electricity when they spin.

When wind turbines are linked in "farms" located where the wind reliably blows, such as the open plains or ocean coasts, they can make enough electricity to power a town or city.

Using the wind to make electricity avoids using coal- or oil-burning power stations, lessening our problems with global warming.

Scientists like Maria Telkes had another Big and Shiny Idea: the sun.
Sun, or solar, energy is "the cleanest and healthiest fuel."
In the 1940s, Telkes, dubbed the Solar Queen, helped design the Dover Sun House, an experimental home.
DOVER SUN HOUSE 1948
It employed special sun-sensitive chemicals that absorbed the sun's energy and then gave off heat or cooling when called upon.
It failed, but that didn't stop Telkes.
"It is the things supposed to be impossible that interest me. I like to do things they say cannot be done."

In 1971, she and her colleagues built Solar One, the first house to generate electricity from the sun using panels made of a special material that changes sunlight into electricity.

Solar panels began turning up in all kinds of places . . . even in outer space, powering satellites!

Cheaper and more efficient solar panels can now be seen on homes everywhere.

Sun-made electricity can work together with regular electricity to provide power day and night; the solar panels generate electricity that is stored in batteries, to be used when the sun is not shining.

Yes, Volta's battery invention is still going strong. Modern scientists have found ways for batteries, tiny and huge, to be more powerful and last longer.

Modern batteries are at the heart of electric cars.
You'd probably be surprised to know electric cars have been around for more than one hundred years.
Thomas Edison had an electric car, of course!

But over time, gasoline-powered cars became faster, more powerful, could travel farther, and were cheaper than electric cars. During the 1960s, electric cars were mostly just curiosities.

The most curious one was the one we sent to the moon. It had a top speed of eight miles an hour and carried astronauts miles from their base.

Time passed, and electric cars improved. By 2012, Tesla Motors (named in honor of Nikola) was selling electric cars that traveled 200 miles on one charge. It ushered in a new era of electric cars, despite its $109,000 price tag.

They have become cheaper, and their range has lengthened. Charging stations—the "gas stations" for electric cars—have become more numerous.

And since they don't burn gasoline, electric cars don't release harmful, climate-warming gases into the environment.

That's good!

Up until now, I've told you how electricity *behaves*, how it is *made*, and what it can *do*, but I haven't told you what it *is*.

To understand that, I must first introduce you to the atom.

Everything is made of atoms. This book, the chair you sit on, the walls of the room, the air you breathe . . . and you!

Yes, you are made of atoms. They are tiny things, too small to be seen with your eyes, not even scrunched-up eyes, or using a magnifying glass, or even with a conventional microscope. Millions can fit within the period at the end of this sentence.

Atoms are made of a neutron, protons, and electrons.

Their number depends on the kind of atom; an atom of oxygen has a different number than an atom of tin.

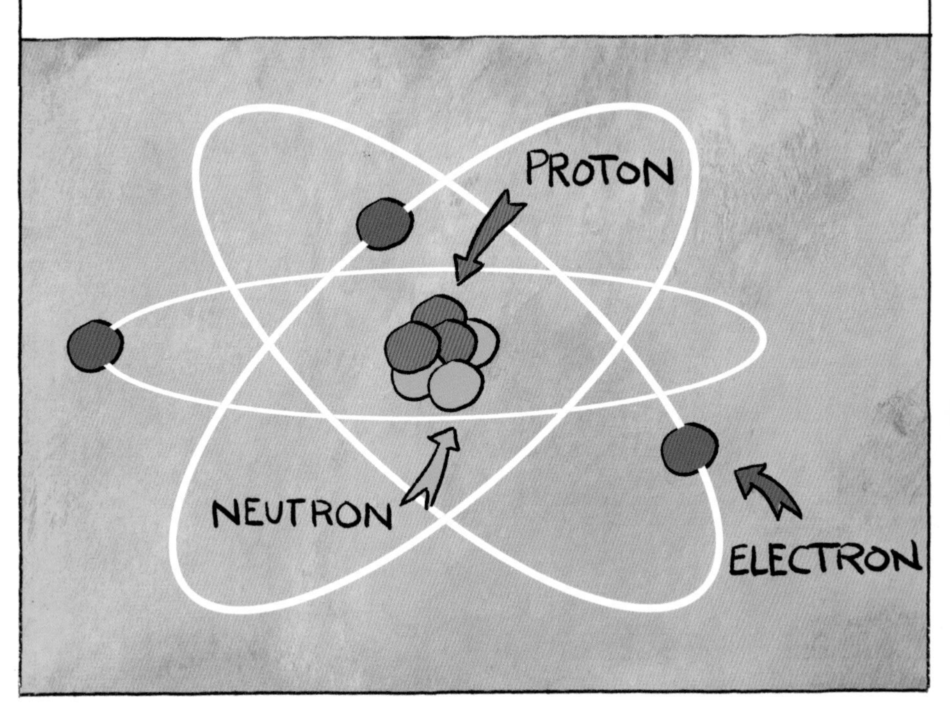

Protons and neutrons huddle together while the electron flies around them, something like how the moon circles Earth.

Neutrons have no electrical charge. Protons have a positive one and electrons a negative one.

Since opposite charges attract, protons and electrons prefer to couple up. That is, there should be an equal number of protons and electrons in an atom.

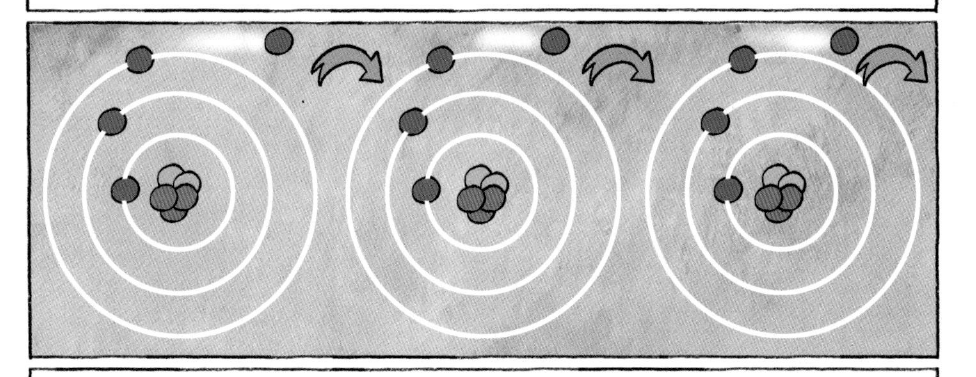

Sometimes an outside force can excite an electron and set it flying off to another atom, where it finds a new proton buddy, pushing out an electron at the new atom in the process.

When bunches of electrons move from atom to atom, electricity is made.

If the outside force is something like a hand rubbing cat fur, the electrons in the fur bounce willy-nilly and make static electricity.

If the outside force is a magnet rotating around copper, the electrons in the copper flow in the same direction, something like a river current.

It is those tiny electrons moving in a current that have given us . . .

electric cars, trains, airplanes, and buses.

Electric scooters. Electric bikes.

Refrigerators, freezers, and fans.

Electric ovens, toasters, mixers, and knives.

Dishwashers, clothes washers, and dryers.

Blowers, mowers, shovels, saws, speakers, and stereos.

Front doors, office doors, and garage doors.

Drills, drivers, and hammers.

Electric printers and watches.

Cell phones and cameras.

Electric thermometers. Electric toothbrushes.

Lights! Incandescent, neon, and LED.

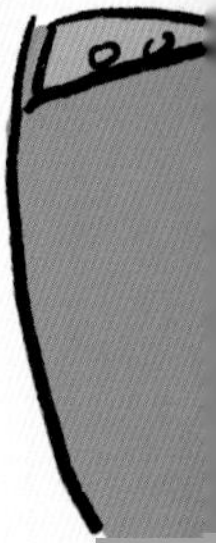

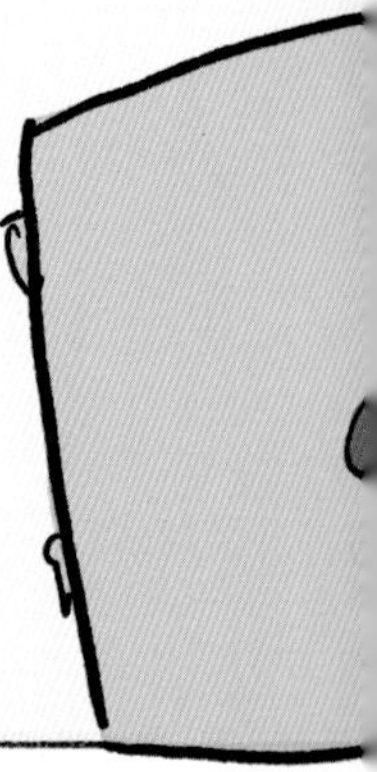

And on, and on, and on . . . all the product of discoveries, thoughts, and ideas, big and small, by men and women, from here and there, over years and years, piled up, one after the other, charging us up and plugging us into Our Electric Life.

Now that's an idea bigger than hair oil on a cyclone!

Byapok!

Hahaha!

# Those Pesky ELECTRONS at WORK

Rubbing amber with a cloth draws off electrons, leaving an abundance of protons on the amber. It can be said the amber now has a positive charge.

As you've read, electrons can do things like attract feathers to amber or shoot sparks off a boy's nose. How does that happen?

Note: Illustrations are merely descriptive and are not scientifically accurate.

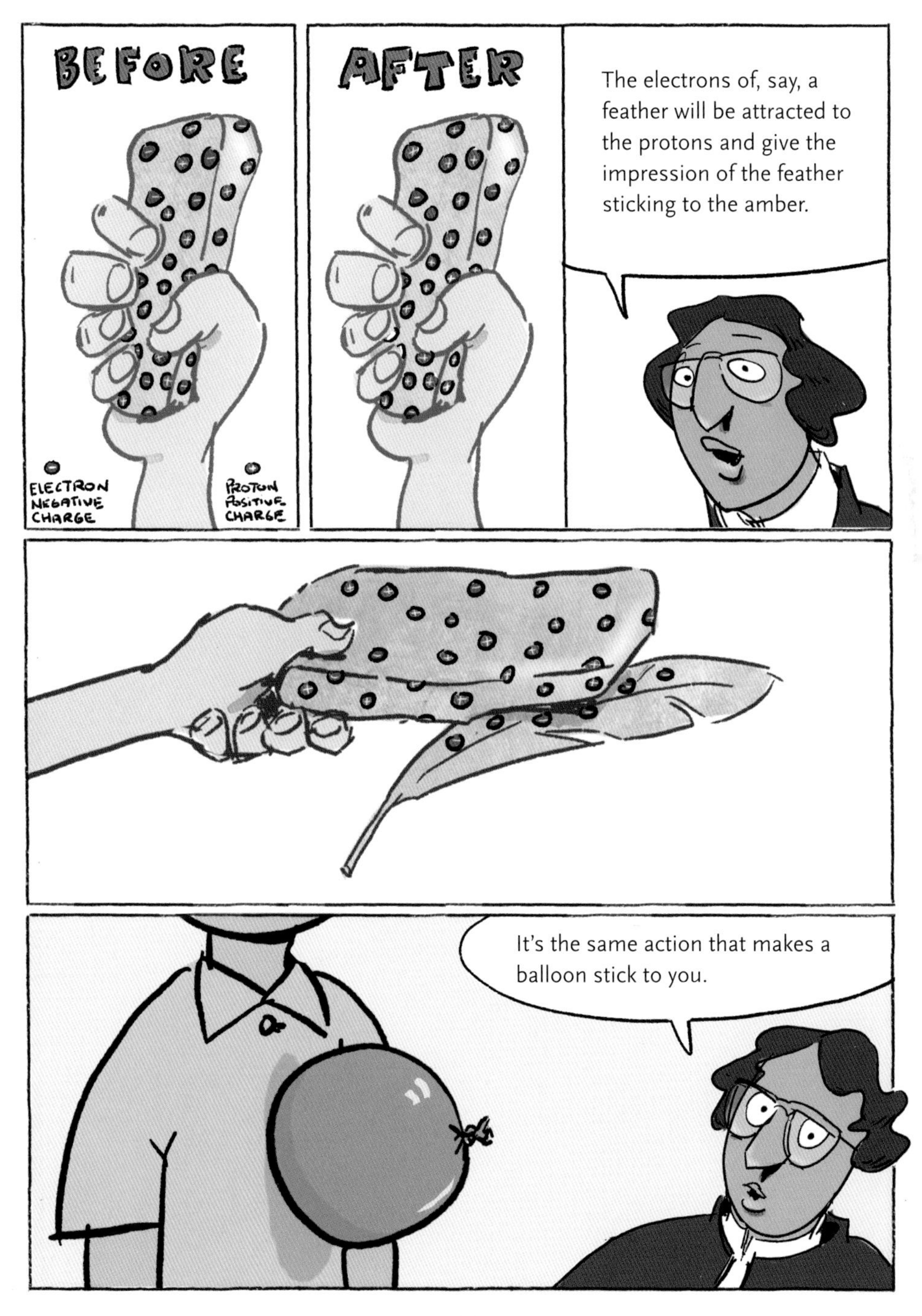
BEFORE
ELECTRON NEGATIVE CHARGE
PROTON POSITIVE CHARGE
AFTER
The electrons of, say, a feather will be attracted to the protons and give the impression of the feather sticking to the amber.
It's the same action that makes a balloon stick to you.

A Hauksbee machine transfers electrons to a Leyden jar, where they wait for a chance to couple with protons.
ELECTRONS
ELECTRONS
ELECTRONS
PROTONS
ELECTRONS
The electrons will rush to protons on a person touching the brass globe, resulting in a shock.

The Flying Boy is charged with electrons with a Hauksbee machine.
The silk ropes don't conduct electricity very well . . .
. . . ensuring most of the charge stays with the boy. The protons on a finger brought close to the boy's nose attracts the electrons and makes a spark.

Sometimes the turbulence in a storm can strip electrons from the rain, snow, or ice in a cloud.
The atmosphere between them acts like an insulator.
The result can be an imbalance of more protons in the top of the cloud and electrons at the bottom. We know protons and electrons want to be together, so if the imbalance is great enough, they unite in a bolt or sheet of lightning.

Sometimes electrons and protons from different clouds make lightning.

When electrons find protons on the ground, lightning will strike downward.

# SELECT TIMELINE

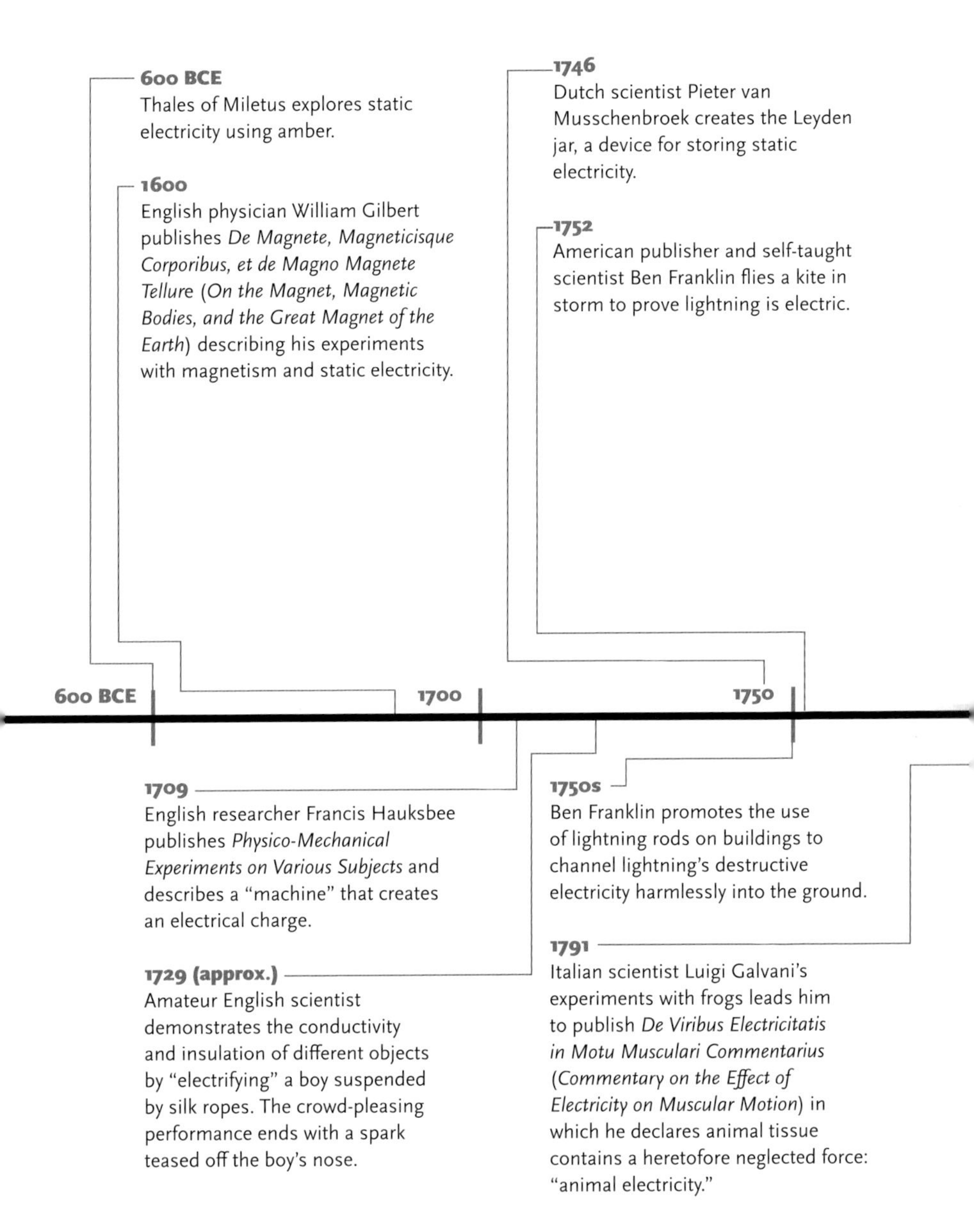

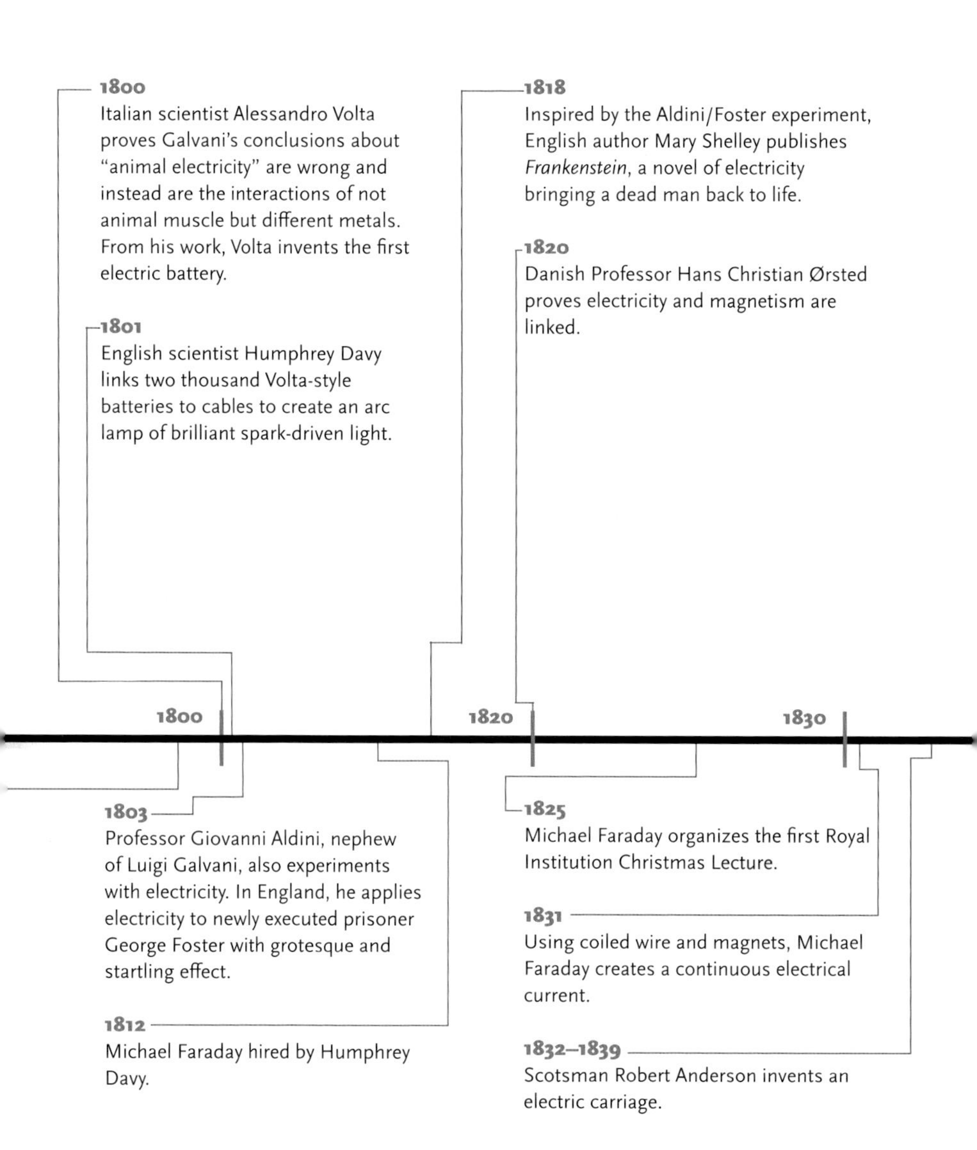
1800
Italian scientist Alessandro Volta proves Galvani's conclusions about "animal electricity" are wrong and instead are the interactions of not animal muscle but different metals. From his work, Volta invents the first electric battery.
1801
English scientist Humphrey Davy links two thousand Volta-style batteries to cables to create an arc lamp of brilliant spark-driven light.
1818
Inspired by the Aldini/Foster experiment, English author Mary Shelley publishes *Frankenstein*, a novel of electricity bringing a dead man back to life.
1820
Danish Professor Hans Christian Ørsted proves electricity and magnetism are linked.
1800
1820
1830
1803
Professor Giovanni Aldini, nephew of Luigi Galvani, also experiments with electricity. In England, he applies electricity to newly executed prisoner George Foster with grotesque and startling effect.
1812
Michael Faraday hired by Humphrey Davy.
1825
Michael Faraday organizes the first Royal Institution Christmas Lecture.
1831
Using coiled wire and magnets, Michael Faraday creates a continuous electrical current.
1832–1839
Scotsman Robert Anderson invents an electric carriage.

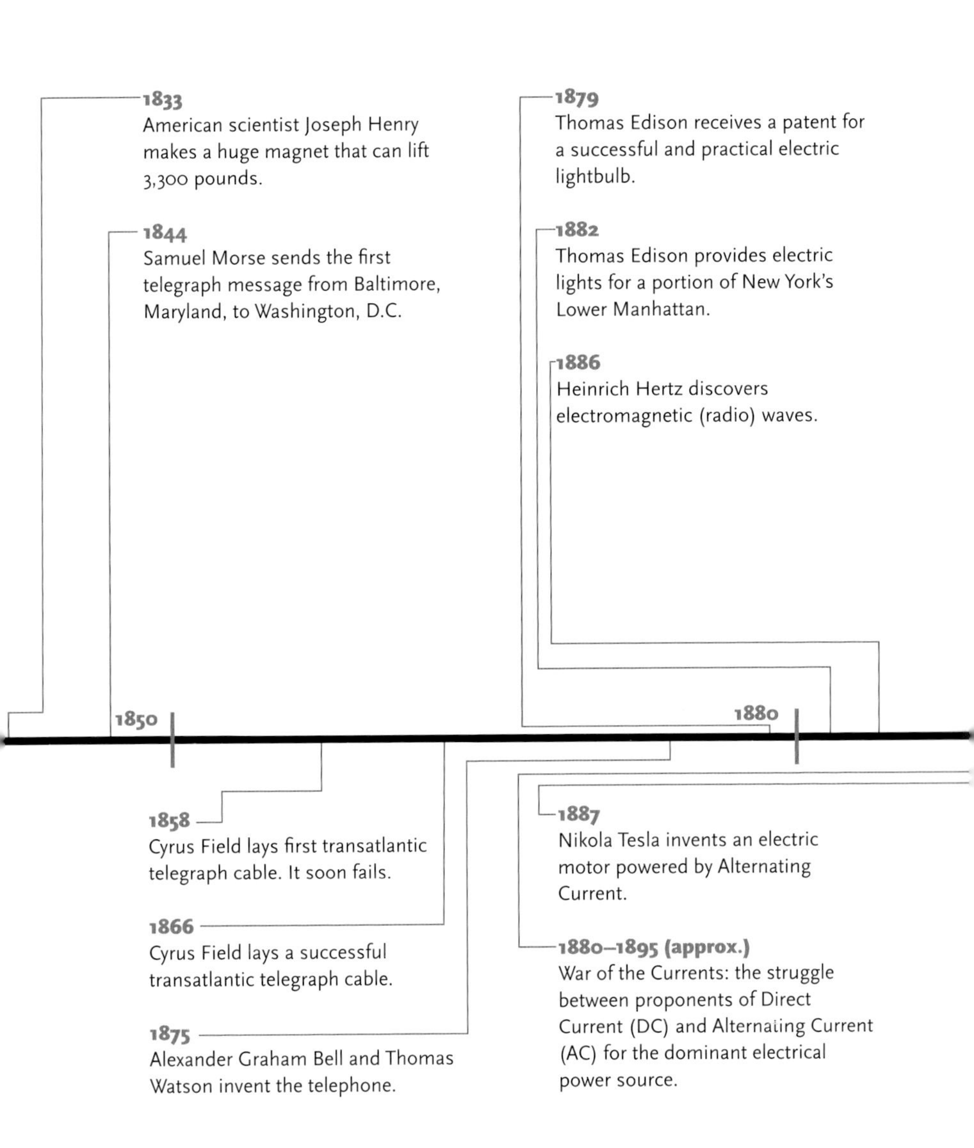

1833
American scientist Joseph Henry makes a huge magnet that can lift 3,300 pounds.
1844
Samuel Morse sends the first telegraph message from Baltimore, Maryland, to Washington, D.C.
1879
Thomas Edison receives a patent for a successful and practical electric lightbulb.
1882
Thomas Edison provides electric lights for a portion of New York's Lower Manhattan.
1886
Heinrich Hertz discovers electromagnetic (radio) waves.
1850
1880
1858
Cyrus Field lays first transatlantic telegraph cable. It soon fails.
1866
Cyrus Field lays a successful transatlantic telegraph cable.
1875
Alexander Graham Bell and Thomas Watson invent the telephone.
1887
Nikola Tesla invents an electric motor powered by Alternating Current.
1880–1895 (approx.)
War of the Currents: the struggle between proponents of Direct Current (DC) and Alternating Current (AC) for the dominant electrical power source.

**1890 (approx.)**
American William Morrison builds an electric wagon. It could carry six people and travel at fourteen miles an hour.

**1894**
English scientist Oliver Lodge uses radio waves to ring a bell.

**1901**
Granville T. Woods receives a patent for the third-rail invention to power electric trains.

**1901**
Guglielmo Marconi sends a radio signal from England to Newfoundland, Canada.

1890 — 1900 — 1920

**1895**
The Niagara Water Falls in New York are used to power dynamos that provide electricity to the city of Buffalo. Its success marks the triumph of AC over DC current for most use.

**1895**
Jagadish Chandra Bose transmits radio wave for about a mile.

**1911**
Dutch physicist Heike Kamerlingh Onnes discovered superconductivity.

**1915**
French physicist Paul Langevin and Russian engineer Constantin Chilowsky invented sonar.

**1919**
Edwin Howard Armstrong developed the standard AM radio receiver.

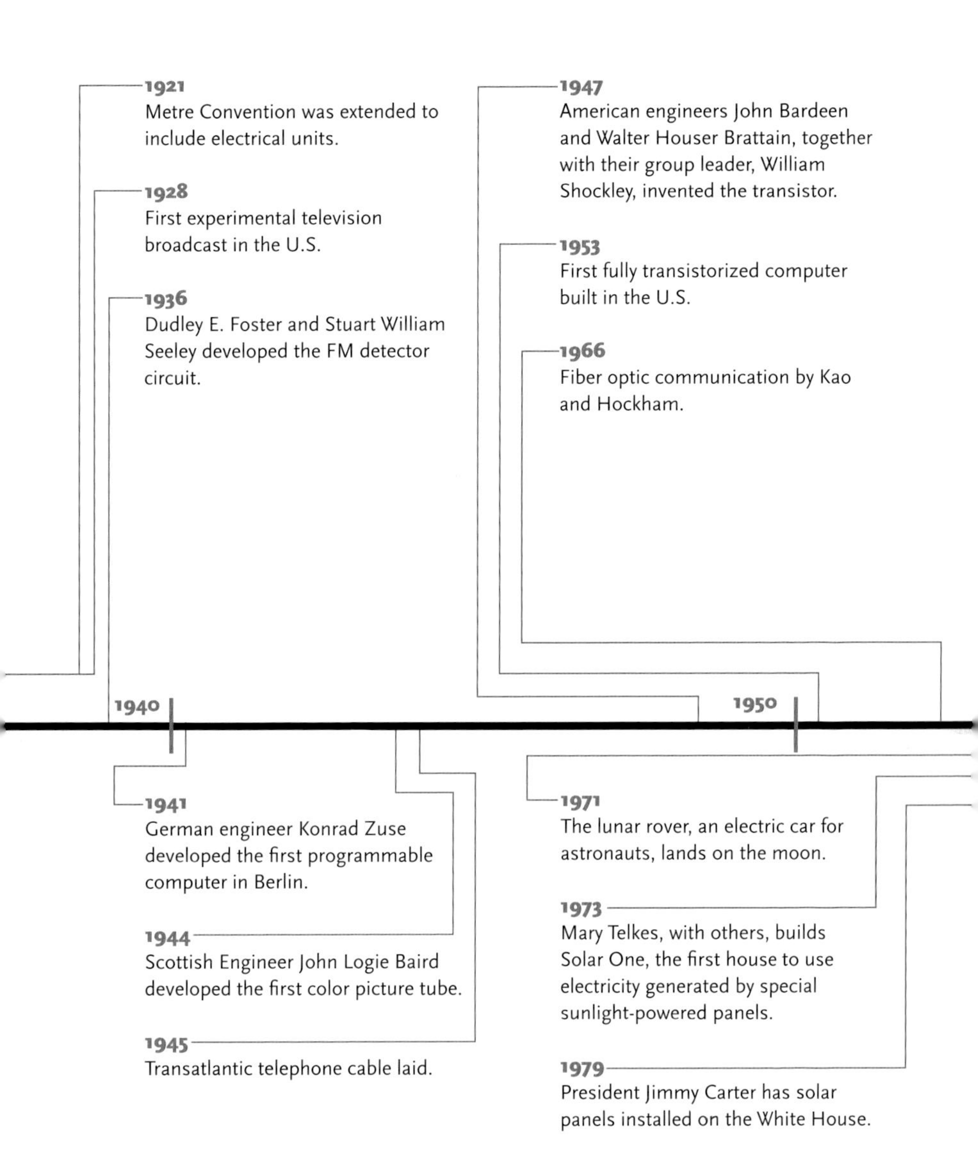

1921
Metre Convention was extended to include electrical units.
1928
First experimental television broadcast in the U.S.
1936
Dudley E. Foster and Stuart William Seeley developed the FM detector circuit.
1947
American engineers John Bardeen and Walter Houser Brattain, together with their group leader, William Shockley, invented the transistor.
1953
First fully transistorized computer built in the U.S.
1966
Fiber optic communication by Kao and Hockham.
1940
1950
1941
German engineer Konrad Zuse developed the first programmable computer in Berlin.
1944
Scottish Engineer John Logie Baird developed the first color picture tube.
1945
Transatlantic telephone cable laid.
1971
The lunar rover, an electric car for astronauts, lands on the moon.
1973
Mary Telkes, with others, builds Solar One, the first house to use electricity generated by special sunlight-powered panels.
1979
President Jimmy Carter has solar panels installed on the White House.

**1981**
The Solar Challenger, the first aircraft to run on solar power, flew across the English Channel from France to the U.K.

President Ronald Reagan ordered the White House solar panels to be removed.

**1991**
First offshore "farm" of electricity-generating turbine windmills built in Denmark.

First onshore "farm" of electricity-generating turbine windmills built in England.

**1996–1999**
General Motors builds the EV1, an electric car. Despite its popularity, GM ends its leasing program, recovers the cars and destroys them.

**1997**
Toyota Prius becomes the world's first mass-produced hybrid electric vehicle. (A car that is powered by both gasoline and electricity.)

**2008**
The all-electric Tesla Roadster is released. Its battery can power it for 250 miles, and it comes with a $100,000 price tag.

**2010**
President Barack Obama requests that solar panels be reinstalled at the White House.

**2016**
More than one million solar panel installations have been completed in the U.S.

1990 2000 2015

# WHO WAS JAGADISH CHANDRA BOSE?

Jagadish Chandra Bose demonstrating his wireless millimeter wave (microwave) experiments at the Royal Institution, London, in January 1897.

A man of wide talents and interests, and a pioneer in both radio technology and plant physiology as well as having a knack for writing science fiction, **Jagadish Chandra Bose** was born in 1858 in Bengal, India (now Bangladesh). The son of a prestigious civil servant, Bose was educated at the finest schools in Calcutta, India, then sent to England to study natural sciences. He returned to India, where he became a professor of physics at Presidency College, the oldest college in Calcutta.

Excited by revelations about wireless communication pioneered by English scientist Oliver Lodge, Bose conducted his own research. By 1895, he was a forerunner in wireless technology and had the technical edge over another researcher of wireless communication, Guglielmo Marconi. But it was Marconi who would go on to complete the first transatlantic radio transmission, receive international fame, and win a Nobel Prize. Few people took note that Marconi's equipment included a radio receiver invented by Bose. (Bose hadn't patented his work, believing restricting inventions to only those who could pay for access to them was destructive to science and the public good.)

Still, some understood Bose's contribution.

"J. C. Bose was at least sixty years ahead of his time," said 1977 Nobel Laureate Sir Nevill Francis Mott.

Bose later shifted his attention to biophysics and studied plants' reaction to different stimuli.

"All around us, the plants are communicating," he said. "We just don't notice it."

Needing a way to measure plant movement, Bose invented a device to detect it within 1/100,000 of an inch.

His research helped improve plant care and pioneered best practices for farmers.

In 1917, he founded the Bose Institute in Calcutta, dedicated to plant research, where he served as director until his death in 1937.

# NOTES

**Page 9**—"smatterers, learned idiots . . . wranglers and perverse little folk." Heilborn, p. 169.

**Page 15**—"struck with such a force that my whole body quivered like someone struck by lightning . . . I thought I was done for." Jonnes, p. 23.

**Page 17**—"universal blow throughout my whole body." Jonnes, p. 27.

**Page 30**—"the most wonderous apparatus that has ever come from the hand of man, not excluding the telescope or steam engine." Jonnes, p. 31.

**Page 34**—"the spark, the light of which was so intense as to resemble the sun . . . a dazzling splendor." Rhodes, p. 176.

**Page 38**—"An attempt should be made to see if electricity . . . has any action of a magnet." Jonnes, p. 36.

**Page 43**—"There were plenty of books there and I read them." Rhodes, p. 181.

**Page 45**—"Convert(ing) magnetism into electricity." Jonnes, p. 39.

**Pages 51**—"What hath God wrought!" Morse and Telegraph.

**Page 56**—"Watson. Come here. I want you." Alexander Graham Bell.

**Page 67**—". . . the same wire that brings the light to you . . . will also bring power and heat . . . you may cook your food," Edison said. Jonnes, p. 56.

**Page 71**—"All our devices and parts . . . were homemade . . . Our men were without central power experience . . . what might happen on turning a big current into the conductors under the streets . . . no one could say." Jonnes, p. 81.

**Page 73**—"They're on!" Jonnes, p. 84.

**Page 73**—"The light was soft, mellow, and grateful to the eye." Jonnes, p. 84.

**Page 75**—"Impractical." King.

**Page 92**—"the cleanest and healthiest fuel." Rinde.

**Page 92**—"It is the things supposed to be impossible that interest me. I like to do things they say cannot be done." Rinde.

# SELECT BIBLIOGRAPHY

## Articles

"15 Simple and Sweet Bengali Phrases." Bilingua.com. See bilingua.io/15-simple-and-sweet bengali-phrases.

"Alexander Graham Bell." Famous Scientists. See www.famousscientists.org/alexander-graham-bell.

Asmelash, Leah. "No, a Black man didn't invent the light bulb. But Lewis Howard Latimer made it better." CNN.com, September 4, 2020. See www.cnn.com/2020/09/04/us/biden-lightbulb-black-man-trnd/index.html.

Blakemore, Erin. "How Twitching Frog Legs Helped Inspire 'Frankenstein.'" *Smithsonian* magazine. December 4, 2015. See www.smithsonianmag.com/smart-news/how-twitching-frog-legs-helped-inspire-frankenstein-180957457.

Bruntland, Terje. "Francis Hauksbee and his Air Pump." The Royal Society Publishing, July 11, 2012. See doi.org/10.1098/rsnr.2012.0023.

Campbell, Barbara. "Tribute Paid to Black Inventor." *New York Times*, April 24, 1975, p. 34. See www.nytimes.com/1975/04/24/archives/tribute-paid-to-black-inventor.html.

Chu, Elizabeth and Tarazano, D. Lawrence. "A Brief History of Solar Panels." *Smithsonian* magazine. See www.smithsonianmag.com/sponsored/brief-history-solar-panels-180972006.

Corazza, Gian Carl. "Marconi's History." Proceedings of IEE, March 4, 1998. See courses.washington.edu/ee420/handouts/marconi.pdf.

"Edison's Electric Light and Power System." ETHW.org. See ethw.org/Edison's_Electric_Light_and_Power_System.

"Electricity Explained: How electricity is generated." U.S. Energy Information Administration, U.S. Government. See www.eia.gov/energyexplained/electricity/how-electricity-is-generated.php.

"Electricity Explained: The science of electricity." U.S. Energy Information Administration, U.S. Government. See www.eia.gov/energyexplained/electricity/the-science-of-electricity.php.

Emerson, D.T. "The Work of Jagadis Chandra Bose: 100 years of mm-wave research." National Radio Astronomy Observatory, February 1998. See hwww.cv.nrao.edu/~emerson/bose/bose.html.

Eschner, Kat. "This 1940s Solar House Powered Innovation and Women in STEM." *Smithsonian* magazine, December 12, 2017. See www.smithsonianmag.com/smart-news/1940s-solar-house-powered-innovation-and-women-stem-180967515.

"Fact Check-Lewis Latimer invented a longer lasting filament for lightbulbs, not the lightbulb itself." Reuters.com, March 5, 2021. See www.reuters.com/article/factcheck-lightbulbs-latimer-idUSL2N2L3237.

*Fantastic Worlds: The Body Electric, Inspiring* Frankenstein. Smithsonian Libraries. See library.si.edu/exhibition/fantastic-worlds/body-electric.

"First transatlantic telegraph cable completed." History.com, July 27, 2018. See www.history.com/this-day-in-history/first-transatlantic-telegraph-cable-completed.

George, Luvenia. "Innovative Lives: Lewis Latimer, Renaissance Man." Lemelson Center, February 1, 1999. See invention.si.edu/innovative-lives-lewis-latimer-1848-1928-renaissance-man.

"Guglielmo Marconi obituary—archive, 1937." Guardian, July 21, 2020. See www.theguardian.com/technology/2020/jul/21/guglielmo-marconi-obituary-archive-1937.

Gupta, Dr. D. P. Sen. "Jagadish Chandra Bose: The Physicist Who Was Forgotten." IEEE Organization. See site.ieee.org/indiacouncil/files/2019/07/p47-p53.pdf.

"Harnessing Niagara." *Tesla: Life and Legacy*. PBS. See www.pbs.org/tesla/ll/ll_niagara.html.

Herres, David. "Francis Hauksbee and static electricity generation." *Tips and Measurement Tips: An EE online resource*, January 23, 2015. See www.testandmeasurementtips.com/hauksbee-generation-static-electricity.

"History of the Electric Car." Department of Energy, U.S. Government, September 15, 2014. See www.energy.gov/articles/history-electric-car.

"History of Solar." Office of Energy Efficiency and Renewable Energy, U.S. Government. See www1.eere.energy.gov/solar/pdfs/solar_timeline.pdf.

"How Electricity Works." Save on Energy. See www.saveonenergy.com/how-electricity-works.

"Jacobi's Motor." Elektrotechnisches Institut (ETI). See www.eti.kit.edu/english/1382.php.

Jorgensen, Timothy J. "Shock value: The life and death story of electricity." Princeton University Press, November 22, 2021. See press.princeton.edu/ideas/shock-value-the-life-and-death-story-of-electricity.

King, Gilbert. "Edison vs. Westinghouse: A Shocking Rivalry," *Smithsonian* magazine, October 11, 2011. See www.smithsonianmag.com/history/edison-vs-westinghouse-a-shocking-rivalry-102146036.

Lantero, Allison. "The War of the Currents: AC vs DC." Department of Energy, US Government, November 18, 2014. See www.energy.gov/articles/war-currents-ac-vs-dc-power.

"Lewis Latimer." Lewis Latimer. See www.lewislatimer.net/fact-fiction.

"Lewis Latimer." National Inventors Hall of Fame. See www.invent.org/inductees/lewis-latimer.

"Morse Code and the Telegraph." History.com, June 6, 2019. See www.history.com/topics/inventions/telegraph.

Matulka, Rebecca and Wood, Daniel. "History of the Light Bulb." Energy.gov, Department of Energy, U.S. Government, November 22, 2013. See www.energy.gov/articles/history-light-bulb.

Nix, Elizabeth. "How Edison, Tesla, and Westinghouse Battled to Electrify America." History.com October 24, 2019. See www.history.com/news/what-was-the-war-of-the-currents.

Padnani, Admisha. "Granville T. Woods." Overlooked, *New York Times*. See www.nytimes.com/interactive/2019/obituaries/granville-t-woods-overlooked.html.

"Pearl Street Station." ETHW.org. See ethw.org/Edison's_Electric_Light_and_Power_System.

Pilkington, Mark. "Sparks of Life." Guardian, October 6, 2004. See www.theguardian.com/education/2004/oct/07/research.highereducation1.

"The Practical Incandescent Light Bulb." Edison Museum. See edisonmuseum.org/content3399.html.

Rife, Patricia. "Lise Meitner." Jewish Woman's Archive. See jwa.org/encyclopedia/article/meitner-lise.

Rinde, Meir. "The Sun Queen and the Skeptic: Building the World's First Solar Houses." Science History Institue, July 14, 2020. See www.sciencehistory.org/distillations/the-sun-queen-and-the-skeptic-building-the-worlds-first-solar-houses.

"Salaries in the 1800s." Career Trend. See careertrend.com/salaries-in-the-1880s-13655312.html.

Shenoy, Gautham. "What's Jagadish Chandra Bose and his hair oil doing in a sci-fi column?" *Factor Daily*, December 2, 2016. See archive.factordaily.com/jc-bose-science-fiction-new-worlds-weekly.

*Shock and Awe*: Episode 1. "Spark." Transcript. TVO. See www.tvo.org/transcript/134049X/shock-and-awe-spark.

*Shock and Awe*: Episode 2. "The Age of Invention." Transcript. TVO. See www.tvo.org/transcript/134050X/shock-and-awe-the-age-of-invention.

*Shock and Awe*: Episode 3. "Revelations and Revolutions." Transcript. TVO. See www.tvo.org/transcript/134051X/shock-and-awe-revelations-and-revolutions.

"Types of Hydropower Plants." Office of Energy Efficiency and Renewable Energy, U.S. Government. See www.energy.gov/eere/water/types-hydropower-plants.

"Types of Hydropower Turbines." Office of Energy Efficiency and Renewable Energy, U.S. Government. See www.energy.gov/eere/water/types-hydropower-turbines.

"What is an atom?" U.S. Nuclear Regulatory Commission, U.S. Government. See www.nrc.gov/reading-rm/basic-ref/students/science-101/what-is-an-atom.html.

"What is electricity?" Wonders of Physics, University of Wisconsin-Madison. See wonders.physics.wisc.edu/what-is-electricity.

Wilson, Kevin. "Worth the Watt: A Brief History of the Electric Car, 1830 to the Present." *Car and Driver*, March 15, 2018. See www.caranddriver.com/features/g15378765/worth-the-watt-a-brief-history-of-the-electric-car-1830-to-present.

"Women's History Month: Women Scientists Shaping Energy." Office of Energy Efficiency and Renewable Energy, U.S. Government, March 19, 2020. See www.energy.gov/eere/articles/women-s-history-month-2020-women-scientists-shaping-energy.

# Books

Bodanis, David. *Electric Universe: The Shocking True Story of Electricity*. New York: Crown, 2005.

Forbes, Nancy & Mahon, Basil. *Faraday, Maxwell, and the Electromagnetic Field.*"Amherst, NY: Prometheus Books, 2014.

Geddes, Patrick. *The Life and Work of Sir Jagadis C. Bose*. London: Longmans, Green & Co, 1920. See en.wikisource.org/wiki/Index:The_Life_and_Work_of_Sir_Jagadis_C._Bose.djvu.

Heilbron, J.L. *Electricity in the 17th and 18th Centuries: A Study of Early Physics*. Mineola, NY: Dover, 1979.

Jonnes, Jill. *Empires of Light: Edison, Tesla, Westinghouse and the Race to Electrify the World.* New York: Random House, 2003.

Rhodes, Richard. *Energy: A Human History*. New York: Simon & Schuster, 2018.

*Sir Jagadis Chunder Bose*. Project Guttenberg. Released July 16, 2007. See www.gutenberg.org/files/22085/22085-h/22085-h.htm.

Sussman, Herbert. *Victorian Technology: Invention, Innovation, and the Rise of the Machine.* Santa Clara, CA: Praeger, 2009.

# Videos

*American Experience*. "Edison."WGBH Educational Foundation, 2015.

*American Experience*. "Tesla." WGBH Educational Foundation, 2015.

*Shock and Awe: The Story of Electricity*. Open University and BBC, Producers. Original Release, 2011.

# AUTHOR'S NOTE

Electricity, in all its manifestations, is so entwined in our lives, so present and ubiquitous, so *common*, that its extraordinary faculties fade into transparency. We no longer notice it—until, of course, we lose it. Whether a hurricane, snowstorm, nor'easter, tornado, or out-of-control station wagon clipping a high-tension pole, the loss of electricity throws us into an existential tizzy.

Fill in the lamentable blank:

"When will the (lights/freezer/heat/AC/TV/cable/Hulu/*power*) come back on?!?"

Even when we try to escape our "modern" world into the boonies, most of us will likely include some kind of an electrical gizmo. Who goes into the woods without a flashlight?

For thousands of years, people were ignorant of electricity. There were no "electric" eels, only odd eels that could deliver an inexplicable *punch*. Lightning? Some kind of monstrous weapon of the gods, perhaps. Then, about 2,800 years ago, people began to have a rudimentary knowledge of its behavior but still viewed it as nothing greater than a kind of parlor trick with floating feathers and sparks leaping off kids' noses.

With the Enlightenment, that astonishing era devoted to logic and science, learned men turned their minds to a more serious inquiry into electricity. (Amazing as it was, the Enlightenment still wasn't welcoming of learned *women*. Or people of color.) Knowledge expanded and accelerated. The invention of electrical devices blossomed, and the telegraph, telephone, and electric light arrived. Amazing inventions all, yet the true revolutionary and transformative invention was the power grid—the idea of an electrical web that could ostensibly deliver electricity anywhere and everywhere to everyone. Thomas Edison envisioned as much.

But Edison's confidence in his own flawlessness led him into backing the wrong technology, direct current (DC). He had famously electrified Lower Manhattan using DC and was invested in its promotion both financially and reputationally. But employing direct current meant constructing power plants *nearly every mile*, a costly requirement that would make electrification financially possible for only densely populated cities. Rural areas would be out of luck. It is at this moment that Nikola Tesla arrived on the scene. He had emigrated from Serbia, bringing a vision of world served by alternating current (AC) and the singular electrical engineering skills to make the vision real. He teamed with businessman George Westinghouse to promote AC electricity with miles and miles of wire connected to a distant, central power station.

The competition between Edison and Westinghouse/Tesla became known as the War of the Currents. The rivalry was bitter. Although best known for his scientific acumen, Edison was a hard-nosed—some say ruthless—businessman. But in the end, the advantages of AC were too much to ignore, and it became the dominant system.

Along the way, Westinghouse stumbled into financial difficulties. Tesla purposely forfeited important patents he had on AC inventions, thus relieving Westinghouse of the requirement to pay Tesla for their use. The grand gesture helped Westinghouse but lost Tesla a mind-boggling fortune. He would die penniless.

The historical verdict on Tesla is still out. Some people champion Tesla as the father of our modern electrical world who *created* what Edison could only *envision*. To others, his reputation is overblown and undeserving. I'm a sucker for a great David versus Goliath story—Tesla and Edison—and come down on Tesla's side. But, hey, I retain an open mind for arguments from the other side.

Tesla, Edison, Faraday, Hertz, and many others contributed to the Big Idea of our All Charged Up civilization, each building atop preceding ideas. It's good to remember that BIG IDEAS are not an end point but just one stop on a continuum of ideas, big and small, that stretch across time. Whether an inspired success or a tragic failure, the ideas are a trail I'll follow in the Big Ideas Series. And, like other trips, the pleasure will not be in the destination but in the journey.

# INDEX